The Ordination of Women

The Priesthood of all Believers
and other Aspects

Expanded Second Edition

By
Pastor Jan Voerman

World rights reserved. This book or any portion thereof may not be copied or reproduced in any form or manner whatever, except as provided by law, without the written permission of the publisher, except by a reviewer who may quote brief passages in a review.

This book was written to provide truthful information in regard to the subject matter covered. The author assumes full responsibility for the accuracy of all facts and quotations as cited in this book. The opinions expressed in this book are the author's personal views and interpretation of the Bible, Spirit of Prophecy, and/or contemporary authors and do not necessarily reflect those of TEACH Services, Inc.

This book is sold with the understanding that the publisher is not engaged in giving spiritual, legal, medical, or other professional advice. If authoritative advice is needed, the reader should seek the counsel of a competent professional.

Cover: Qingwa/BigStock.com

2nd Edition
Copyright © 2014 Jan Voerman
Copyright © 2014 TEACH Services, Inc.
ISBN-13: 978-1-4796-0249-0 (Paperback)
ISBN-13: 978-1-4796-0175-2 (ePub)
ISBN-13: 978-1-4796-0176-9 (Mobi)
Library of Congress Control Number: 2014934778

Published by

All scripture quotations, unless otherwise indicated, are taken from the King James Version Bible. Public domain.

Scripture quotations marked (ASV) are taken from the American Standard Version Bible. Public domain.

Scripture quotations marked (NEB) are taken from The New English Bible.
Copyright © 1961, 1970 by Oxford University Press and Cambridge University Press.
Used by permission. All rights reserved.

Scripture quotations marked (BV) are taken from The Berkeley Version in Modern English.
Copyright © 1959 by Zondervan Publishing House.
Used by permission. All rights reserved.

Revised Standard Version (RSV) of the Bible, Copyright © 1952 [2nd edition, 1971] by the Division of Christian Education of the National Council of the Churches of Christ in the United States of America.
Used by permission. All rights reserved.

Other books in English written by Jan Voerman: *The Hidden Agenda*; *Secret Messages in the Church*; and *Ellen White and The Trinity*.

Jan Voerman also writes books in Dutch, German, Spanish and Danish.

Table of Contents

Introduction. 7

Chapter 1   A Threefold Foundation 11

Chapter 2   Does Christ's Priestly Ministry
Sanction Women's Ordination? 17

Chapter 3   Ellen White's Testimony 26

Chapter 4   Parental Crisis. 29

Chapter 5   Double Task 31

Chapter 6   Adam and Eve: Clothed as Priests? 33

Chapter 7   The Husband: Head or Caretaker? 40

Chapter 8   The Biblical Principle of the
Priesthood of all Believers 47

Chapter 9   Not a Teacher 55

Chapter 10   Leaders in the Church 58

Chapter 11   A Solemn Responsibility. 60

Chapter 12   Ministry of Women. 62

Chapter 13   Ordination vs. the Laying on of Hands. 67

Chapter 14   A Striking Parallel. 70

Chapter 15   Differences. 73

Chapter 15   The Possibility of Creating a Schism 77

Chapter 17   Home and Church 79

Chapter 18   Neither Male nor Female. 82

Chapter 19   A Biblical Concept of Inspiration 85

Chapter 20   Reputable Women in the Bible 90

Chapter 21   Junia, a Woman Apostle?. 100

Chapter 22   Phoebe, A Woman Church Leader?. 108

Chapter 23   Women Who Can Manage a Church? 115

Chapter 24   Women Not Permitted to Speak? 117

Chapter 25   Bible Truth or Cultural Values? 121

Bibliography 127

Introduction

If you ask a fellow church member if he or she thinks a certain woman in your church should be made pastor, you may see some sparks fly. It doesn't matter if the member or woman in question is conservative or liberal; this issue causes heat on both sides. Rarely does an issue cause controversy in such a broad segment of the church body. Almost everyone can relate to this issue and almost everyone has an opinion about it.

Some questions we might ask are: Can a woman be considered a spiritual leader after the role of priest in the Bible, as a man apparently is? Do we see women actually performing the role of priest in the Bible? Do we really see women leaders in the Bible exhibiting the same characteristics as the role of priest? Did God intend that women should serve as priests or pastors? What does divine revelation have to say? Perhaps we should also compare the roles of biblical priest and pastor to provide a ground for the resolution of this issue. What exactly are the roles of priest and pastor? Are they the same or do they differ?

Although we, as Seventh-day Adventist Christians, may decide to place the Bible and Spirit of Prophecy first as our authorities for any significant world church-based action, we must also consider the fact that in modern times the general society has swung far wide of these authorities in every area of life. Christians, and even Seventh-day Adventist Christians, who have been known in the not-so-far-distant past as the "people of the Book," have retrograded along with the rest. Today it doesn't seem to be easy for us to accept the "narrower" frame of reference that the Bible seems to offer. You may ask: How could the Bible be considered a narrow frame of reference? Despite the obvious answer to this question, many view the Bible as a book of history and stories, full of antiquated and outdated precepts written down by mere men, who are as human as everyone else, including us.

We now live in a secular world, where the divine does not often intervene, at least on a broadly accepted scale. Our authorities tend to be philosophers, psychologists, psychiatrists, professors, and scientists. Research, not divine inspiration or revelation, is the basis for truth, which is always relative and dependent upon our role and specific situation. Furthermore, each of us is sole judge and authority in our particular situation. Women have been emancipated since the middle of the nineteenth century, there is cultural diversity with full and legal acceptance of creed and color, and now there is also sexual emancipation. The Jews, for instance, lived in a much more prescribed society with respect to social, economic, and religious practices.

These facts, however, do not justify an acceptance of the status quo, but rather, a recognition of the fact that as freedom has increased, so has sin and suffering. Perhaps there is need to re-examine God's original plan for men and women, and listen to what our church fathers have to say about the roles of men and women in society and the church. We have seen a disintegration of family life, and dysfunction of every type is rampant. These conditions have caused much pain and grief in the lives of non-Christians and Christians alike. Faith-based living should exhibit a difference and a greater contentment. Although peace and order seem to be difficult to achieve in these times, we know that God has promised to bless us according to our faith. A return to our founding principles may be the very prescription we need, not more "freedom." There is true liberty only in Christ. We might be surprised but pleased to find that, upon full commitment to biblical truth, we would actually achieve what we have longed for. Unfortunately, "freedom" is a deception—a satanic trap we fall into when we avoid what we know we should do.

For every sincerely committed Christian, God's holy Word is the ultimate source of knowledge, and the standard against which all things he believes and teaches should be tested.

As His intentional revelation and authority on earth, the Scriptures express His holy and unerring will. God's people should not try to explain the Scriptures in such a way as to reconcile contemporary social and cultural views with its precepts. Nor should the Scriptures be adjusted and adapted to popular principles. On the contrary, society should reconcile itself with God's holy and unchanging word. The rules and principles of the Bible are universal and far elevated above every society and above any culture. If we are to prove God's promises to us, we must follow, exemplify, and defend the principles laid out in His Word.

Thus, when we study a subject such as the ordination of women, we should not be guided by social or cultural prevailing standards that could noticeably differ from place to place. Our only reliable guide to understanding God's purpose for men and women is the unchanging word of God. It is true that we do not always find in the Bible a direct and straightforward answer to all our questions. Nowhere in the Scriptures do we read a plain: "Thou shalt not baptize little children" or "Thou shalt keep the Saturday as God's Sabbath." Nor do we read: "Thou shalt not ordain women." However, sincere seekers of truth who search and study God's holy word with reverence will find that its principles will lead to a clear and convincing biblical point of view. Proverbs 3:5 says: "Trust in the Lord with all thine heart; and lean not unto thine own understanding." This verse expresses the first principle of Bible study. If we do not wrest the scripture to fit our own narrow purpose, but instead trust God and the Holy Spirit to reveal the truth, we may expect that the truth we should know will be made clear to us. If our hearts are sincere, and if we are prepared to do God's will, we shall receive understanding. As is promised, we "shall know of the doctrine, whether it be of God" (John 7:17).

As a church we have been brave enough to defend our biblical viewpoint against the opinion of the great majority regarding the day of rest, the mortality of the soul, the millennium, and other important biblical truths. The courage to stand alone, grounded by our love of God and the truth of His Word, becomes an indispensable and holy power that binds us together. When we adopt another course by not following God's word exclusively, but prevaricate, heeding contemporary insights, customs, habits, and social developments, then as a church, we will irrevocably lose our power and unity, together with our special task and calling in this world.

Chapter 1

A Threefold Foundation

In our modern age, in many lands of the civilized world, women are encouraged more than ever to take part in the economic process. Women are often promoted to posts of responsibility and leadership. The popular viewpoint in many countries is that women are equal to men; that is, except for the obvious sexual difference, there is no difference between them with respect to ability or role. As Christians we should observe and practice respect and appreciation for women, without any form of discrimination. However, since the Bible is the standard for every true Christian, we should always measure our lives and opinions against it and act accordingly.

The apostles Paul and Peter testify similarly about the position of women in relationship to men. Since these chosen apostles were inspired workers of God, the biblical statement certainly applies that "the testimony of two men is true" (John 8:17), and also that "in the mouth of two or three witnesses every word may be established" (Matt. 18:16b). Thus every sincere Christian should consider the testimonies of these two apostles to be trustworthy.

The apostle Paul, in 1 Corinthians 14:34, places himself on the absolute platform of God's law: "They [women] are commanded to be under obedience, as also saith the law." "They must, as the Law says, take a secondary place" (Berkeley Version). "But let them be in subjection, as also saith the law" (ASV). "They have no license to speak, but should keep their place as the law directs" (NEB). Paul does not refer to cultural or social insight or public opinion; he refers directly to the law.

Paul comments upon the relationship a woman should have to a man in 1 Corinthians 11:8, 9: "For the man is not of the woman; but the woman of the man. Neither was the man created for the woman; but the woman for the man." Here Paul refers to the Creation of mankind, placing himself undeniably on the ground of God's authority as the Creator of mankind. In 1 Timothy 2:13, 14 Paul again refers to the Creation, and also to the fall: "For Adam was first formed, then Eve. And Adam was not deceived, but the woman being deceived was in the transgression."

Thus, there is a threefold immovable foundation on which the relationship of man to woman and woman to man rests. These three fundamental realities are the law, Creation, and the fall. It is evident that Paul does not refer to the law of the ten commandments. The apostle clearly refers here to another law, spoken by God at the beginning, right after the fall. In consequence of the fall, God spoke to Adam and Eve and specified a law of life governing the relationship of a man and a woman: "Unto the woman he said, I will greatly multiply thy sorrow and thy conception; in sorrow thou shalt bring forth children; and thy desire shall be to thy husband, and he shall rule over thee" (Gen. 3:16).

Here we have a clear "Thus saith the Lord." God Himself spoke to Eve. He did not speak through an angel or any other being. This is a clear and direct Word of the Lord personally addressed to Eve. We might ask: Is this law given only to a restricted group of people (Eve's descendants), who observe a certain culture? Was this law enforced only during the period of the Old Testament, after which it was nailed to the cross? Or should we perhaps believe that this law was only in force until Paul wrote to the Galatians: "There is neither male nor female: for ye are all one in Christ Jesus" (Gal. 3:28)?

If it is supposed that this law has ended, then there should also have been a release for women from the pain and sorrow of childbearing. Women would also have been released from the desire to please and obey their husbands. Or shall we suppose that only a small part of God's command, "and he shall rule over thee," has come to an end? Omission of one and not all parts of the law of life would be inconsistent, and God is certainly not inconsistent. Rather, His law is eternal.

No, God has spoken. He has made His will clear to men. Since we live in a secular world where nothing seems to stand out in clear and distinct lines and where human reasoning is strong and often accepted as qualifying, we may be tempted to question God's spoken word and not recognize it as authoritative above all else. Ellen White stresses the right attitude we should adopt toward

God's spoken word. "God has made known His will, and it is folly for man to question that which has gone out of His lips. After Infinite Wisdom has spoken, there can be no doubtful questions for man to settle, no wavering possibilities for him to adjust. All that is required of him is a frank, earnest concurrence in the expressed will of God. Obedience is the highest dictate of reason as well as of conscience" (White, *The Acts of the Apostles*, p. 506).

How was this significant issue regarded and performed in the early church? Research shows that women were ordained only as deaconesses. The church historian, Joseph Bingham, explains: "Yet we are not to imagine, that this consecration gave them any power to execute any part of the sacerdotal office, or do the duties of the sacred function" (Bingham, *Origines Ecclesiasticae, or the Antiquities of the Christian Church and Other Works*, vol. 1, p. 254). In fact, the title of the section that this quote appears in is titled "Not Consecrated to any Office of the Priesthood" (Ibid.). He adds: "Women were always forbidden to perform any such offices as those. Therefore the author of the Constitutions calls it a heathenish practice to ordain women priests, … for the Christian law allowed no such custom. Some heretics, indeed, as Tertullian (Constit. Apost. Lib. iii, c. 9.) observes, allowed women to teach, and exercise, and administer baptism; but all this, he says, was against the rule (Tertul. De Praescript. C. 41.) of the Apostle" (Ibid.).

Thus we see that in the early church there was consistency with respect to this issue. Only a small apostate group had women leaders. Bingham records: "Epiphanius brings the charge particularly against the Pepuzians, which were a branch of the Montanists, 'that they made women bishops, and women presbyters, abusing that passage of the Apostle, 'In Christ Jesus there is neither male nor female,' to put some colour upon their practice. He charges it also upon the Collyridians (Epiph. Haer. 49, Pepuzian, n. 2 …), 'that they did … *use women to sacrifice to the Virgin Mary*;' where, it is observed, that the charge is double: 1st, that they gave divine worship to the holy Virgin; and 2dly, that they used women priests in their service. Against these he has a particular dissertation, wherein he shows at large that no woman, from the foundation of the world, was ever ordained to offer sacrifice, or perform any solemn service (Id. Haer. 78. Antidicomarianit. n. 23.) of the Church; which, if it had been allowed to any, would certainly have been granted to the Virgin Mary herself, who was so highly favoured of God. But neither she nor any other woman had ever the priest's office committed to them" (Ibid., pp. 254, 255).

These passages from Bingham's writings affirm that the early church was in accord with the law of life given to Adam and Eve by God, the same law that was reinforced by Paul, and the law that also, by inheritance and example, was given to all men and women after them.

In the early church bishops and presbyters (elders) were usually called "priests" (sacerdotes). Although all believers were conceived as spiritual priests, forming a universal priesthood, bishops and elders were regarded in a more special sense.

At an early stage, the ministry of bishops and elders was compared with the Old Testament priesthood ministry, and it was viewed in its light. Bishops and elders, as part of their duties, presented the emblems of Christ's sacrifice at the Lord's altar or table as offerings to the people, and thus, they were viewed as priests, not in the sense of the concept of a universal priesthood of all believers, but by virtue of their office and ministry.

There was in the apostolic church not much difference between bishops and elders. "The presbyters or elders, or bishops were of equal rank, having a just and true parity" (Fallows, T*he Popular and Critical Bible Encyclopaedia*, vol. III, p. 1370).

Presbyters and bishops ministered as ordained officers publicly in holy things pertaining to God, with power and authority, according to God's appointment.

The priests in the Old Testament performed the ministry of reconciliation in the temple. In the New Testament the ministry of reconciliation is given to the ministers or pastors of the gospel as "ambassadors for Christ," as God's mouthpiece, beseeching the people, "in Christ's stead, be ye reconciled to God" (2 Cor. 5:20).

The Greek word for ambassador is presbeuo from the base of presbuteros. It means "to be the elder or eldest; to rank before, take precedence of others. To be an ambassador or go as one; to treat or negotiate as one" (Bullinger, *A Critical Lexicon and Concordance to the English and Greek New Testament*, p. 48).

The word ambassador is significant. "In the OT the idea behind the words translated 'ambassador' (generally mal'akh) is that of going or being sent, and of this the etymological equivalent in the NT is not 'ambassador' but 'apostle' (apostolos, 'one sent forth'); but both the OT terms and the NT apostolos have to be understood in the light of use and context rather than of derivation. In this way they acquire a richer content, of which the chief component ideas are the bearing of a message, the dealing, in a representative character, with those to whom one is sent, and the solemn investiture, before starting out, with a delegated authority sufficient for the task (cf. Gal 1:15–17) ... There is no very marked difference between 'ambassador' and 'apostle'" (Hastings, *Dictionary of the Apostolic Church*, vol. 1, p. 52).

The Old Testament Hebrew word mal'akh, corresponding to the New Testament Greek word presbeuo (ambassador), was also used in a similar way to denote a priest as being God's ambassador or messenger (Mal. 2:7).

Furthermore, "The English word 'priest' is simply a contraction of the Latin presbyter, ... a name of office in the early Christian church" (Cheyne, *Encyclopaedia Biblica*, columns 3833, 3837).

Thus we note a clear link between priest and presbyter, or elder, while there is also a link between ambassador and apostle, and since the Greek word presbeuo (ambassador) is from presbuteros, there is also a clear link with presbyter (elder) or bishop.

In the Old Testament a priest is denoted as being God's messenger or ambassador, while in the New Testament apostles, presbyters (elders), and bishops are in a similar way God's ambassadors, sharing the ministry of reconciliation.

No wonder that in the early church presbyters and bishops were called priests. Being the mouth of God and of the congregation, they offered up spiritual sacrifices, thanksgivings, prayers, and praises, and they made intercession to God. In God's name they blessed the people, advocated the remission of sins and spiritual regeneration, and baptized people. Bishops and presbyters, in their priestly, or sacerdotal role, officiated in the service remembering Christ's death, offering the emblems of Christ's broken body and shed blood to the people. The deacons, in the early church, were never allowed to perform this act of priestly ministry and offer these oblations of bread and wine at the altar. It was always a peculiar act of the presbyter's office. (cf. Bingham, *Origines Ecclesiasticae, or the Antiquities of the Christian Church and Other Works*, vol. 1, pp. 203–206). A deacon "does not bless or baptize or offer ... but that, when a bishop or presbyter has offered, he gives [the sacrament] to the people, not as a priest (iereus) but as one who ministers to the priests" (Hastings, *Encyclopaedia of Religion and Ethics*, vol. VIII, p. 665). Bishops and presbyters occupied a priestly, or sacerdotal, office. They were called and ordained to govern and to rule the church in the name of God with delegated authority.

When we consider these characteristics, we readily recognize that also a contemporary minister or pastor of the church could be, in this sense, called a priest, for he performs similar priestly duties that were reserved for the bishops and presbyters in the early church. The titles bishop and pastor were soon regarded as being similar. "The word 'pastor' or 'shepherd'... was often applied to bishops by later writers (e.g., Apost. *Const.* ii. 1)" (Ibid., p. 662).

The Greek word presbeuo in 2 Corinthians 5:20 is "employed by Paul to designate the nature and dignity of the office of a minister of the Gospel. They are representatives of Christ, because in the name of Jesus Christ the King of kings they declare his will to men, and transact the important business of their reconciliation with God (Eph. vi:20)" (Fallows, *The Popular and Critical Bible Encyclopaedia and Scriptural Dictionary*, vol. I, p. 94).

"Paul ... in 2 Cor 5:20 includes with himself, all ministers of the gospel, as 'ambassadors ... on behalf of Christ,' commissioned by Him, as their sovereign Lord, with the ministry of reconciling the world to God. The Bible contains no finer characterization of the exalted and spiritual nature of the minister's vocation as the representative of Jesus Christ, the King of kings, and Saviour of the world" (Orr, *The International Bible Encyclopaedia*, vol. I, p. 115).

A pastor or minister is a leading shepherd who watches, feeds, and heals the flock. In the Bible this office is applied to God and to Christ (Ps. 23:1; Isa. 40:11; John 10:14; 1 Peter 22:25). Human shepherds or pastors, such as priests and prophets, are God's representatives on earth, appointed by Him as leaders to feed the flock (Jer. 23:1–4, 11; Eph. 4:11; Eze. 34:2). Pastors or shepherds should, like the biblical bishops, elders, or presbyters, feed the flock and take the oversight thereof according to Christ's model as the chief Shepherd (1 Peter 5:1–4).

Although literally not identical in all parts and aspects, there is a clear spiritual relation between the ministry of the priests in the Old Testament and the priestly ministry of bishops, presbyters, and pastors in the New Testament as the divinely ordained and appointed shepherds of the flock. However, there is no evidence nor any example of female shepherds who were appointed and solemnly ordained and invested as such with authority to perform the priestly ministry.

Chapter 2

Does Christ's Priestly Ministry Sanction Women's Ordination?

For our understanding and true meaning of the priestly ministry of Christ in the heavenly sanctuary, we are dependent upon the revelations of God as written down by His servants. Paul, in particular, deals with this topic in his epistle to the Hebrews, evidently written before he wrote his epistles to Timothy and Titus. According to Ellen White, Paul was divinely instructed.

Paul, in his ministry, "had taught the people 'not with enticing words of man's wisdom, but in demonstration of the Spirit and of power.' The truths that he proclaimed had been revealed to him by the Holy Spirit" (White, *The Acts of the Apostles*, p. 402).

"He had received the truths of the gospel direct from heaven, and throughout his ministry he maintained a vital connection with heavenly agencies. He had been taught by God regarding the binding of unnecessary burdens ... Paul knew the mind of the Spirit of God ... and took a firm and unyielding position which brought to the churches freedom from Jewish rites and ceremonies" (Ibid., p. 200). "Paul was an inspired apostle. The truths he taught to others he had received 'by revelation'" (Ibid., p. 302).

"He claimed no wisdom of his own, but acknowledged that divine power alone had enabled him to present the truth in a manner pleasing to God.

United with Christ, the greatest of all teachers, Paul had been enabled to communicate lessons of divine wisdom, which met the necessities of all classes, and which were to apply at all times, in all places, and under all conditions" (Ibid., p. 303). Paul "had received abundant revelations from God" (White, *The Paulson Collection of Ellen G. White Letters*, p. 243).

Thus, we should be assured that the apostle Paul was accurately instructed with respect to the issue in question. He certainly would know how Christ's priestly ministry and the New Testament principle of the priesthood of all believers would fit together and precisely relate to the position and service of women in the church. When the Bible reveals the abiding truth for mankind, then, if somehow we come to a conclusion that is not entirely in harmony with Paul's teaching, we may be sure that such a conclusion is not only at variance with Paul's counsel, but also in defiance of God's revelation and instruction.

The apostle Paul, as we have seen, was very specific in his teaching about the position of a woman, placing himself on a sure threefold platform of God's Law, Creation, and the fall. We could be inclined to bypass this distinct truth, because we might feel that Paul's perspective of the subordinate position of women is not entirely in harmony with Christ's priestly ministry and the principle of the priesthood of all believers. However, such a feeling does not demonstrate that Paul in this teaching was dubious or culturally influenced. Rather, it reveals that *our* understanding is not quite correct; therefore, we should study the subject more carefully.

Furthermore, Paul clearly specified the essential requirements for a position of leadership in the church. Therefore, we should carefully consider if there is any indication that the apostle also included women in this prescription for leadership.

If Christ's priestly ministry would make it possible for women to minister as leaders in the church, equivalent to the ministry of men, we should certainly find some evidence in Paul's teaching for such an important variation, since this particular apostle deals specifically with both subjects: Christ's priestly ministry and the ordination of leaders in the church.

Many well-meaning preachers argue in good faith that there is no basis in the New Testament for recognizing any difference between men and women with regard to serving the church in any position. These preachers are bold and convincing, often offering desirable arguments in favor of this point of view. With due respect, however, it should be realized that sincere Christians will demand that such arguments be in harmony with the Bible, without neglecting certain passages. We should, therefore, investigate whether the functional equality of men and women is a valid biblical concept.

If we refer to Christ's priestly ministry to justify this egalitarian position of men and women, we should consider that the inspired and enlightened apostles understood what they wrote about. We may be assured that the apostle Paul, who deals with this subject in his letter to the Hebrews, certainly presented this topic without any contradiction with the teachings in his other letters. The apostles were the first builders and organizers of the New Testament Church. The Holy Spirit guided them in a special way to establish new churches, to preach the truth, to reveal the will of God, and to make right decisions.

Thus, if we assert that Christ's priestly ministry justifies that women should serve in leading positions of responsibility in the church, just as men, then certainly the apostles, including Paul in particular, should be aware of this notable fact. Or should we conclude that this is new light, not revealed to the apostles? If this is the case, the question arises: How can we still regard the Bible as a complete revelation of God's will and as the standard of all teaching for all men of all ages? No, Paul could not have been ignorant of such a weighty issue. Therefore, we can safely accept the supposition that the apostle Paul knew how Christ's priestly ministry relates to the position and service of women in the church because he wrote authoritatively by divine revelation about Christ's heavenly ministry, the assignment and position of a woman, and the requirements of those leading the church. Note how the apostle, under divine inspiration, first specifies very clearly the responsibility, task, and place of a woman and then continues to present the necessary qualities of a church leader, elder or bishop.

Paul wrote: "Let the woman learn in silence with all subjection. But I suffer not a woman to teach, nor to usurp authority over the man, but to be in silence. For Adam was first formed, then Eve. And Adam was not deceived, but the woman being deceived was in the transgression. Notwithstanding she shall be saved in childbearing, if they continue in faith and charity and holiness with sobriety" (1 Tim. 2:11–15).

Having described the relationship between man and woman so clearly and specifically, Paul then goes on to describe the qualities of a leader who is to exercise authority over the church. Will the apostle give us an indication that women can also be responsible leaders in the church? But wouldn't that be contradictory? After this description of a woman's position, can we expect that the apostle would consider women for leading positions of authority in the church? In harmony with his previous statement, it is no wonder that the apostle speaks only in terms of male church leaders, such as the "husband of one wife" and "If a man know not how to rule his own house, how shall he take care of the church of God?" No, we do not find any hint of a female church leader. In this passage that outlines the requirements for male church leaders, the apostle exclusively uses the pronoun "he" and never "she:" For example, the passage specifies: "If a man desire the office of a bishop, he desireth a good work" (1 Tim. 3:1). It does *not* specify: If a man *or woman* desire the office of a bishop, he *or she* desireth a good work.

In accordance with the instructions given to Timothy, Paul clearly directs Titus to ordain masculine elders in every city of Crete: "For this cause left I thee in Crete, that thou shouldest set in order the things that are wanting, and ordain elders in every city, as I had appointed thee" (Titus 1:5). The Greek word *presbuterous* clearly signifies older men.

A good question we might ask is: Were there men in every city who met Paul's requirements for ordination? When Paul wrote to Titus, the various churches on Crete were very young and not well organized. Considering the situation, it might be relevant to question whether competent, acceptable men could be easily found. Crete is not a large island; it is safe to assume that Titus had to care for some small groups that included few men who were prepared for leadership. But the experienced apostle Paul, who certainly knew the problems Titus would face, does *not* in any way suggest that if there is not a competent man, he should look for a dedicated woman. On the contrary, Paul clearly charged Titus to ordain men in every city, without providing any exception to this rule. We find this policy to be in complete harmony with Paul's inspired teaching in all of his various letters.

Thus, the Bible simply indicates that the office of a bishop, overseer, presbyter, or elder would be filled by a man. The context refers to men only and the Greek words used for these officers are masculine. We are assured that when "ordaining suitable men to act as officers, the apostles held to the high standards of leadership outlined in the Old Testament Scriptures" (White, *The Acts of the Apostles*, p. 95). Thus, as to church leadership, neither Christ's priestly ministry, nor the principle of the priesthood of all believers, has given rise to a significant change.

We should fully trust the Bible, just as it reads. Ellen White wrote: "If men would but take the Bible as it reads, if there were no false teachers to mislead and confuse their minds, a work would be accomplished that would make angels glad and that would bring into the fold of Christ thousands upon thousands who are now wandering in error" (*The Great Controversy*, p. 599). Should we not study the Bible with a humble and teachable spirit to obtain true knowledge? If we insist on having our own way, trying to find in the Bible some support to back up our own viewpoint, won't the truth be obscured by our viewpoint? This insistence really constitutes resistance to the Holy Spirit. We must remain open and teachable.

When we operate faithfully in harmony with Biblical principles, then blessings and appreciation are to be expected. Thus also, when an elder rules well, he will be much honored and appreciated. "Let the elders [older men—the Greek is clearly masculine] that rule well be counted worthy of double honor, especially they who labor in the word and doctrine" (1 Tim. 5:17).

This issue of masculine leaders in the church is not only important, but far-reaching in its results. Therefore, not only should we have clear insight on the matter, but we should *expect* that God would not leave us in doubt or ignorance with respect to this serious matter. Thus we should *expect* that if women were to be included as leaders of the church, some clear hint in that direction would certainly have been given. But that is not the case. As sincere Bible students we are admonished to take God's Word as it is; misconstruing it for any reason is not to our advantage. In fact, misconstruing it could result in serious harmful consequences.

Some people try to explain that when men are mentioned in the Bible, it should be understood that according to linguistic usage, women are not excluded but rather, included, and thus it is no problem to ordain women elders also. In general or common cases this point of women's inclusion is sometimes valid, but the appointment of elders or bishops as leaders in the church is not at all a common matter that applies to everyone. It is a clearly restricted and confined appointment of a selective and specifically qualifying function, and in a case like this, where characterizing qualities are at stake, women are not tacitly included when men are mentioned. As we look at the context where behavior and position in the church is addressed, it is clear that Paul deals with men and women separately and not collectively.

With regard to women, the apostle states very clearly and specifically: "She shall be saved in childbearing, if they continue in faith and charity and holiness with sobriety" (1 Tim. 2:15). Paul's statement indicates where a woman's main duties and responsibilities lie. The statement ends a passage reviewing the appropriate demeanor and role for a woman in the church, based on the relationship between Adam and Eve with respect to both the Creation and the fall, and it is followed directly by Paul's outline of the requirements for male church leadership.

Note how, for instance, a few commentaries react to this biblical statement:

> In making provision for the birth and nurture of children God has entrusted a great honor and privilege to womankind. When

woman fulfills her trust faithfully, by channeling her energies into the creation of a happy, orderly home, she will not only be called blessed by her husband and children but will also receive the approbation of the Lord. Salvation cannot be separated from a person's day-by-day relation to the responsibilities of life. To forsake or neglect her God-appointed sphere of activity for other pursuits may result in unhappiness and loss. Paul urges all women to do their duty as faithful mothers and to recognize man's God-given responsibility of leadership in the home and in the church. God has given to both men and women special qualifications for accomplishing their individual tasks, and both will find their greatest happiness in filling their assigned places with a spirit of love, devotion, and faithful service. (White, *The SDA Bible Commentary*, vol. 7, p. 296)

By her faithfully performing her part in doing and suffering what God has assigned to her—viz., child-bearing and home duties, her sphere, as distinguished from public teaching, not hers, but man's" (vv. 11, 12). 'In this home sphere, not ordinarily in public service for the kingdom of God, she will be saved on the same terms as all others-viz., by living faith.' (Jamieson, *A Commentary Critical, Experimental and Practical*, vol. VI, p. 486)

In child-bearing—The woman's office is here described, in the contrast with the duty of teaching and governing: *bringing forth and training children*. (Bengel, *New Testament Word Studies*, vol. 2, p. 515)

It is here implied that woman is to find her right sphere in the relations of motherhood ... Her sphere is in the home life; her destiny lies in the faithful discharge of its duties. (Spence, *The*

Pulpit Commentary, vol. 21, p. 42)

In childbearing, i.e. by keeping faithfully and simply to her allotted sphere as wife and mother. (Dummelow, *A Commentary on the Holy Bible*, p. 997)

The priority of Adam's creation is thus a testimony for the order of God that the man should lead and rule for all times ... The woman was and should be in the relation of dependency to the man, from which it follows that her status should not be that of a leader or teacher in the Church ... the home, the family, motherhood is woman's proper sphere of activity. Every normal woman should enter holy wedlock, become a mother, and rear her children, if God grants her the gift of babies of her own. That is woman's highest calling; for this God has given her physical and mental gifts. (Kretzmann, *The Popular Commentary of the Bible*, vol. II, pp. 377, 378)

Childbearing, rather than public teaching or the direction of affairs, is woman's primary function, duty, privilege and dignity. (Nicoll, *The Expositor's Greek Testament*, vol. IV, p. 110)

He (Paul) means that God has given to them (women) in place of the Christian ministry reserved for men another office in the Church, in the faithful discharge of which they are to work out their salvation – that of peopling the Church by bearing and training children to be citizens of God's kingdom on earth. (Gore, *A New Commentary on Holy Scripture Including the Apocrypha*, p. 584)

What are we to think of these commentaries? They are, of course, not on the same authoritative level as the Spirit of Prophecy comments are, but it is, nevertheless, interesting to note what they have to say on this prominent issue. Are they all wrong, or perhaps outdated? Can we learn something from these comments? Could we, perhaps, after careful study of this subject, agree that they are in harmony with the will and order of God as revealed by Paul's teaching?

As a church we are richly blessed with the gift of prophecy. We should consider Ellen White's counsel not only unique, truthful, and inspired but also superior to any commentary. In harmony with Paul's statement, a few short quotations from Ellen White's writings are certainly valuable to consider in this context.

Chapter 3

Ellen White's Testimony

Many passages by Ellen White illuminate the importance of the work and duty of the mother. The following quotes are taken from a variety of issues of *Good Health* magazine during the year 1880.

God-appointed work. "But the Christian mother has her God-appointed work, which she will not neglect if she is closely connected with God and imbued with his Spirit… The mother's work is given her of God, to bring up her children in the nurture and admonition of the Lord" (White, "Appeal to Mothers," *Good Health*, January 1, 1880).

Too many burdens. "The mother is frequently overtaxed; too many burdens are allowed to rest upon her … The constant inquiry of every one should be, What is duty? What shall I do to benefit my children and society, and to glorify God?" (Ibid., February 1, 1880).

Influence. "The mother's daily influence upon her children is preparing them for eternal life or death. She exercises a power in her home more decisive than the minister in the desk, or even the king upon his throne" (White, "The Work of Parents," *Good Health*, March 1, 1880).

Result of faithful lessons. "When Samuel shall receive the crown of glory, he will wave it in honor before the throne, and gladly acknowledge that the faithful lessons of his mother, through the merits of Christ, have crowned him with immortal glory" (Ibid.).

Strongest power for good. "Next to God, the mother's power for good is the strongest known on earth" (Ibid.). "I would impress upon mothers that women are accountable for the talents God has entrusted to them. They may engage in missionary work at home, in their families. Their influence is fully equal to that of the husband and father. The most elevated work for woman is the molding of the character of her children after the divine pattern" (White, "The Mother's Influence," *Good Health*, April 1, 1880).

Influence on the church. "The church will bless her because she has educated and developed talent that will be of the highest value. She gives to the church, men and women who will not flinch from duty however taxing. If Christian mothers had always done their work with fidelity, there would not now be so many church trials on account of disorderly members. Mothers are forming the characters that compose the church of God. When I see a church in trial, its members self-willed, heady, high minded, self-sufficient, not subject to the voice of the church, I am led to fear that their mothers were unfaithful in their early training" (Ibid.).

A responsibility, paramount to everything else. "God has given the mother, in the education of her children, a responsibility paramount to everything else" (White, "Influence of Woman," *Good Health*, June 1, 1880). "If she does this work to glorify God, she will not follow the popular path, and will have to stand in defiance of popular customs" (Ibid.). "The mother's nursery is her kingdom" (White, "The Duties of Parents in Educating Their Children," *Good Health*, July 1, 1880). "All the tact and cultivated skill of the mother will be called into requisition if she rules with God-fearing wisdom. She will not turn her children over to hired help, or leave them to obtain a street education" (Ibid.).

Meeting God's standard. "Mothers, shall our precious time be worse than wasted in work and hurry … while but a limited time is improved in educating and disciplining our children? Our hands are on the cradle that rocks the world. Shall our children become what they may be, and what God would have them be? Shall we meet God's standard, revealed to us in his word, or shall our efforts be employed to meet the world's standard?" (Ibid.).

Much faithful, earnest, persevering labor. "Little does the mother realize that her influence in the judicious training of her children reaches with such power through the vicissitudes of this life, stretching forward into the future, immortal life. To fashion a character after the heavenly model requires much faithful, earnest, persevering labor; but it will pay, for God is a rewarder of all well-directed labor in securing the salvation of souls" (Ibid.).

If we carefully consider these passages, we can better understand Paul's statement. The duty of a mother in training her children is, without doubt, a very serious matter. Satan knows that when he can keep mothers busy with other things at the expense of faithfully performing God's appointed work, he will succeed in obtaining control over the children and upset families, churches, and society. How important and often undervalued is the right position of the mother.

In these days, since many mothers have a job outside the home, the proper education of the children is often neglected and we reap the sad results. Why are children often so unruly? Why do many youth leave the church? Why is there among the young people so much criminality and rebellion?

If mothers aspire to a career for themselves, whether in the church or in society, it should be seriously questioned if such an ambition is really in line with God's will, and it must be realized that the occupation of a responsible position will not always turn out to be as beneficial as might be expected.

Consider the sad story of Brigitte, as told in a Dutch daily paper, *De Telegraaf*, December 2, 1995. The important catchwords in Brigitte's story are without doubt: *working parents, loneliness, divorce*. Brigitte is a heroin-whore. She explained that she does not use drugs just for fun but to suppress her feelings. What are the feelings that have influenced her so negatively? She tells that she has always felt very lonely because her parents were working and she had no brothers or sisters. Her parents had little time for her and they also had insufficient time for each other. There was no happy home and at last her parents divorced. Brigitte was happy to have a horse and she sought comfort with the horse she liked so much. However, as a result of the divorce, the horse had to be sold, so she had to give up even the horse that was so dear to her. Brigitte walked away from home and at last her life ended up being wasted.

It does not always happen so dramatically, but there is certainly a lesson for us all. What did Brigitte's parents gain? Would you like to be in their shoes? Was it wise for both parents to work? Is it a good thing for both parents to build up economic security? In cases like this, even if we are apparently successful, and with all we have accomplished, we are often at last forced to admit before God's throne that we have lost everything.

Chapter 4

Parental Crisis

A few years ago an Adventist couple visited us complaining about their two children. These children did not listen, were unruly, self-willed, and followed their own way. Is it any wonder these children were so unmanageable? Father and mother both worked and when their two children came home from school there was no one to guide them. They could take what they wanted and do what they liked, so they were used to following their own way. When both parents came home in the evening, they were busy preparing food and doing other necessary home duties. It is quite clear that their two children did not receive the attention they needed so urgently.

How beneficial when Paul's and Ellen White's inspired words concerning the position and duty of women were taken to heart and more closely followed.

The British International Newspaper *The Guardian* published some interesting articles in September 1991 about the crisis of parenthood. Richard Whitfield, PhD, a prominent British scholar, writer, and social scientist, and chair of the National Family Trust, explained that there is a great crisis in parental care. There is an alarming deterioration of unconditional love. He spoke with a number of school principals, who told him that the children with problems were usually those who did not receive sufficient attention, because both parents worked. These children often felt lonely, were rebellious, and showed antisocial and disorderly behavior.

On a television program presented by Cees Grimbergen, titled "Vesuvius, I or my child," and televised by the IKON (Interchurch Broadcast Netherlands) on the television station Netherlands 1 on January 18, 1996, a number of people revealed their parental problems. The opening words were: "It looks so attractive, a young woman with husband, children and a job. She looks charming and she divides her time so well, but the combination of all tasks often results in prostration. A working mother has to deal with many problems."

Professor T. Knijn, chief of staff of social sciences at the University of Utrecht, explained that for mothers, the results of full time work are often disastrous. There is a great crisis in the education of their children, due to a lack of appropriate parenting. Serious problems, such as criminality among young people, have greatly increased. Children are not properly cared for. They do not receive the quality of love they need so badly, because both parents are working and too busy.

It is quite obvious from the examples above, and many more that any of us could cite or find around us every day, that both Paul's teaching and Ellen White's counsel regarding the duties of a woman, are even more urgent and relevant in this modern age. If a woman plans to accept a job, she should carefully consider that it should not absorb all her time and energy at the expense of her home duties. Should we follow in the footsteps of this world by promoting women's leadership in the church, thus charging them with a twofold, heavy responsibility—that of the church and that of their family? Let us be courageous enough to return to the vital biblical principle encouraging women not to neglect in any way, their duty to care for and educate their children for eternity.

Chapter 5

Double Task

Is it a small and easy task to educate children in the ways of the Lord? Not at all. It is a work of great responsibility paramount to everything else, which requires much faithful, earnest, persevering labor. Is it a small and easy task to be in a position of leadership in the church? Not at all. It is a work of great responsibility that, equally, also requires much patience and faithful, earnest, persevering labor.

Ellen White warns*:* "The mother is frequently overtaxed; too many burdens are allowed to rest upon her" (White, "Appeal to Mothers," *Good Health*, February 1, 1880). Is it fair to overburden a woman with a double task of great responsibility? Yet this is often done at the expense of health, or with insufficient attention given to one or the other task, or both.

Shouldn't we be most thankful to our all-wise heavenly Father for inspiring the apostle Paul by the Holy Spirit to teach and specify that women are *not* called to be ordained to occupy positions of authority and leadership in the church?

If it is God's appointed work that a woman, as her principal task, should train and educate her children faithfully and perform her duties in the family circle, could we then expect the Holy Spirit to call women and provide them with gifts to be responsible leaders in the church with full ecclesiastical authority?

Was it a matter of chance when in the upper room, where both men and women were assembled, that a man was chosen in place of Judas, or was this choice the Holy Spirit's leading? The Bible informs us that the number of names together were about 120 (Acts 1:15). Here was a good opportunity to appoint a dedicated woman, but it did not happen; two men were appointed, not one man and one woman. "Joseph called Barsabas, who was surnamed Justus, and Matthias" were appointed (Acts 1:23). The assembly prayed and asked God: "shew whether of these two thou hast chosen … and the lot fell upon Matthias; and he was numbered with the eleven apostles" (verses 24–26).

But if a dedicated woman is unmarried, would it not then be possible for her to be an ordained leader in the church? Being single, however, is not very likely. The desire of a woman is to a husband (Gen. 3:16). Thus, if single this year, she may possibly be married next year, and occupied with family responsibilities. Even so, the Bible specifies clearly that a church leader should be a man. "If a man desire the office of a bishop, he … must be … the husband of one wife … one that ruleth well his own house" (1 Tim. 3:1-4). A bishop or elder must display a high moral standard. His personal experience of a good marriage enables him to better understand family problems in the church; being a good ruler of his own house fits him to be a responsible leader in the church.

It is true that some women in the Bible occupied important positions, but if there is no clear example nor any suggestion that a woman—whether single, married or without children—was, or could be an ordained leader in the church, we should be very careful *not* to make the wrong decision when confronted with this issue, especially when the general consensus favors women's ordination.

The teachings of the Bible apply to *all* men and *all* women in *all* ages. It is obvious that the position and duties of women have been clearly specified in the Bible. There is evidence that only men are called and chosen to be leaders in the church. Why try to explain these few relevant passages in some other way? Is such a course going to prove profitable?

Chapter 6

Adam and Eve: Clothed as Priests?

After the fall God made coats of skins and clothed Adam and Eve (Gen. 3:21). A number of intelligent men see in this divine act a clear relation to a priestly role. They point out that the rare occasions in the Old Testament when God dressed humans, or commanded to do so, are always connected with the dressing of priests. In their vigorous argumentation, much emphasis is laid on the use of identical words. The Hebrew words *asah*, make (this verb is used in many contexts); *labash* (in its hifil form regarded as a technical term), to dress priests; and *kethoneth*, (priestly) coat or garment, are used in Genesis 3:21. Therefore, they conclude that both Adam and Eve were equally dressed as priests.

Although the priests were not clothed with coats of skins but with white linen and costly apparel, they point out that the skin of the burnt offering was set apart as a gift for the officiating priest (Lev. 7:8). They conclude that since God clothed the first human couple with coats of skins, a gift strictly reserved for priests, that Eve should also be recognized as priest alongside Adam. And so, it is asserted that men as well as women may claim the intended priestly role and be equally ordained.

There is no doubt that this divine act of clothing the first human couple is significant with a special lesson attached to it. However, should we believe that by this divine act Adam and Eve were equally clothed as priests? Is this a correct biblical understanding and interpretation? Can it be justified in light of other Scripture passages and adequately defended with sound biblical arguments?

But what was the *reason* that God made coats of skins and clothed Adam and Eve? Was it to demonstrate their priesthood, or was it for some other purpose? John Peter Lange notes: "They are on the point of being compelled to leave Paradise; they need now a stronger clothing for their entrance upon the climate of the outer land" (Lange, *Genesis or the First Book of Moses*, p. 240). Albert Barnes remarks: "Now God makes necessary provision for man's physical well-being. The covering that man had made for himself was inadequate … He furnished protection against the rigors of climate which would be encountered outside of the garden" (Barnes, *Exposition on Genesis in 2 Volumes*, vol. I, p. 178).

Paul E. Kretzmann observes that Adam and Eve were to wear the coats of skins "as a covering for their nakedness and as a protection against the rigors of a changed climate" (Kretzmann, *The Popular Commentary of the Bible, Old Testament*, vol. 1, p. 10).

Ellen White, commenting on the act of clothing, points out that, "The air, which had hitherto been of a mild and uniform temperature, seemed to chill the guilty pair. The love and peace which had been theirs was gone, and in its place they felt a sense of sin, a dread of the future, a nakedness of soul.… The atmosphere, once so mild and uniform in temperature, was now subject to marked changes, and the Lord mercifully provided them with a garment of skins as a protection from the extremes of heat and cold" (White, *Patriarchs and Prophets*, pp. 57, 61). "The atmosphere was changed. It was no longer unvarying as before the transgression. God clothed them with coats of skins to protect them from the sense of chilliness and then of heat to which they were exposed" (White, *The Story of Redemption*, p. 46).

As to the reason of this act of clothing it is interesting to note that several Bible commentators share, with similar words, Ellen White's explanation. Now, in order to come to a sound biblical conclusion as to whether Adam and Eve were clothed as priests or whether the clothing was simple for protection, we should carefully consider the following points.

1. Ellen White's clear explanation as to why God clothed Adam and Eve is very valuable and should not be overlooked. It is significant that she mentions a changed climate without any mention of the priesthood. Was the change of atmosphere of more value than Adam and Eve's priesthood? If the priestly office was involved in this divine act,

we certainly would consider it important enough to expect her to have made some reference to it, since her writings are always characterized with deep thoughts and much background information of the historical biblical events. That she does not speak about an equal priesthood of Adam and Eve should make us think.

2. Although the act of clothing, due to a changed atmosphere, is in itself described with identical words of dressing the priests, the *purpose* and *reason* of the clothing is not identical. It is clearly *different*; therefore, there is no solid ground for a sound comparison. Thus, we should realize that the same use of words does not necessarily mean that exactly the same act is involved with a same or similar result and purpose.

3. Apart from very specific, technical terms we should not cherish the illusion that significant events or acts that stand on their own are each described with different words, for that would make the vocabulary almost endless. It should be clear that things, events, or acts that have no bearing on each other are often described with similar, identical words, and we must be careful not to draw wrong conclusions. To illustrate this, let's examine the Bible story of the chief butler who told his dream to Joseph. He said: "And Pharaoh's cup was in my hand: and I took the grapes, and pressed them into Pharaoh's cup, and I gave the cup into Pharaoh's hand" (Gen. 40:11). The cup of the king was a very special and valuable object. It was often regarded as a symbol of dignity and magic. The Hebrew word used for Pharaoh's cup in the Genesis account is *kos*. Then, there is the story of a rich and poor man as told by Nathan to David. We read: "But the poor man had nothing, save one little ewe lamb … it did eat of his own meat, and drank of his own cup, and lay in his bosom" (2 Sam. 12:3). Exactly the same word for cup (*kos*) is used in this story. Should we assume that both stories have some bearing on each other? Should we assume that although the man was poor, he must have been a king? That certainly would be uncalled for. Thus, we must be careful in suggesting that Adam and Eve were clothed as priests just because a few identical words are used.

4. It should be noted that the words *labash* (to dress or clothe) and *kethoneth* (coat or garment) are not only used, literally or figuratively,

with regard to the priesthood, as is suggested. Even with the clothing of humans, where action of God is involved, the word *labash* is also used outside of a priestly context. Job, in his affliction, addressed God as follows: "Thou hast clothed me with skin and flesh" (Job 10:11). And in Job 8:22 we read: "They that hate thee shall be clothed with shame." Another figurative example is God's judgment over His rebellious people is found in Ezekiel 7:27: "The king shall mourn, and the prince shall be clothed with desolation, and the hands of the people of the land shall be troubled: I will do unto them after their way." Also the word *kethoneth* (coat, garment) is used without a priestly context: "Israel [Jacob] loved Joseph more than all his children … and he made him a coat of many colours" (Gen. 37:3). When David fled from his son Absalom the Bible tells us that "Hushai the Archite came to meet him with his coat rent, and earth upon his head" (2 Sam. 15:32). Job in his great distress said, "By the great force of my disease is my garment changed: it bindeth me about as the collar of my coat" (Job 30:18). Another example is Tamar who was loved and defiled by Amnon. We read: "And she had a garment of divers colours upon her: for with such robes were the king's daughters that were virgins apparelled" (2 Sam. 13:18). Thus, since the words *labash* and *kethoneth* are not always used in a priestly context, literally or figuratively, it should be regarded as possible that this is also the case with the clothing of Adam and Eve as recorded in Genesis 3:21.

5. If the change of atmosphere is the reason for the divine act of clothing as Ellen White clearly indicates, then it should be regarded as uncalled for to conclude that Adam and Eve, in a special sense, were equally dressed as priests, for this particular ministry didn't have anything to do with a changed climate but with a holy office that was not equally set apart for everyone, as the Bible clearly teaches.

6. It is important to realize that if God had only clothed one and left the other unprotected against the chilliness of the changed atmosphere, it would have spoiled His character with partiality and discrimination. That Eve was also clothed cannot have, therefore, any sound bearing on her supposed priesthood for there was no other choice than to clothe her also. Thus, it is absolutely impossible to assume on this act

of clothing that Adam and Eve were equally dressed as priests since this equal treatment was inevitable according to God's character.

7. Contrary to the clothing of Adam and Eve, we should note that a choice was possible as to the office of the priesthood. In the earliest times the *firstborn son* was chosen to the priesthood (White, *The Desire of Ages*, p. 51, emphasis added). "In early times *the father* was the ruler and priest of his own family" (White, *Patriarchs and Prophets*, p. 141, emphasis added). "In the earliest times *every man* was the priest of his own household." (Ibid., p. 350, emphasis added). Later on in history, God chose the Levites instead of the firstborn to serve in the tabernacle and Aaron and his sons were chosen to minister in the priest's office (Num. 3:12; 8:18, 19; Exod. 28:1). "The bestowal upon Aaron and his house of the priestly office ... had formerly devolved upon the *first-born son* of every family" (White, *Patriarchs and Prophets*, p. 395, emphasis added). Thus, it should be clear that the office of the priesthood was never intended for everyone, men and women alike, but reserved for certain men only. No wonder that we do not find any example in the Bible of a woman priest.

8. The priests received several things as a compensation for their service in the temple. Leslie Hardinge writes: "The remuneration of the priests was precisely prescribed by the Lord, and was to be derived from several sources" (Hardinge, *With Jesus in His Sanctuary*, p. 274). Hardinge presents a list of things the priests received for their service, including "parts of specified offerings, such as the shewbread, meal-offerings, and the designated flesh of burnt-, peace-, and trespass-offerings" (Ibid). Among the compensations a priest received was "the skin of the burnt offering which he hath offered" as recorded in Leviticus 7:8, while the next two verses specify the compensations for their service of the meat offering. Should we now conclude that there is a clear priestly bearing on God's act of clothing Adam and Eve with coats of skins and assume that they were clothed as priests because the priests received the skin of the burnt offering as a reward for their service?

Some problems with this comparative assertion are that Adam and Eve did not do any service to receive their coats of skins while the priests received the skins as a compensation for their service, and the priests were not to wear coats of skins as a typical priestly tunic, for they were to wear a white linen garment woven in one piece (White, *Patriarchs and Prophets*, p. 350). The priestly wardrobe were made of rich materials according to God's design "for glory and for beauty" (Exod. 28:2, 40). Furthermore, some allude to the clothing of Adam and Eve with skins as symbolic of Christ's righteousness, which cannot be said of the skins the priests received as a reward for their service because Christ's righteousness cannot be received as compensation for service. Only the white linen priestly garments reflect Christ's righteousness, which were provided free to the priesthood as part of their office. In ancient times skins were also used to make bags, liquid bottles, music instruments, shoes, parchment, and other common things and so the skins the priests received could serve these different purposes as well. Could there ever be then a priestly comparison possible with Adam and Eve's act of clothing?

9. It should be noted that the context of Genesis 3:21 does not say a word about Adam and Eve being clothed into a priestly role or office while in the other intended examples of dressing by God or by His command, this is clearly pointed out (Exod. 28:41; 29:1, 8; 40:13, 14; Lev. 7:34, 35; 8:1–13; Ps. 132:16). We should, therefore, be very careful not to read something into a passage that is not really there. Even if a certain Bible passage, on the surface, appears to justify a certain thought, we should be very careful not to make hasty or unwarranted conclusions.

In light of these points, it should be clear that Adam and Eve were not clothed as priests. The Bible teaches that the priesthood was not for everyone but was reserved for appointed men only.

There is, nevertheless, in this act of God's clothing of Adam and Eve, a spiritual lesson. Every child of God will be clothed with Christ's righteousness and is expected to reflect God's character. Like the children of Israel were, in a spiritual sense, through faith and obedience, part of God's kingdom of priests, as a holy nation (Exod. 19:5, 6), so were Adam and Eve also, in the same sense, part of God's kingdom. Through faith in the gospel of Jesus Christ, men and women of all nations are, in a general sense, equally part of the spiritual priesthood of all believers when they are dressed with Christ's righteousness and not with the fig leaves of their own making.

Ellen White comments on this: "The Lord Jesus Christ has prepared a covering—the robe of His own righteousness—that He will put on every repenting, believing soul who by faith will receive it. Said John, 'Behold the Lamb of God, which taketh away the sin of the world' (John 1:29). Sin is the transgression of the law. Christ died to make it possible for every man to have his sins taken away.

"A fig-leaf apron will never cover our nakedness. Sin must be taken away, and the garment of Christ's righteousness must cover the transgressor of God's law. Then when the Lord looks upon the believing sinner, He sees, not the fig leaves covering him, but Christ's own robe of righteousness, which is perfect obedience to the law of Jehovah. Man has hidden his nakedness, not under a covering of fig leaves, but under the robe of Christ's righteousness" (White, *The Upward Look*, p. 378).

As we conclude this chapter, we must observe that Eve can only be regarded as priest in a spiritual sense just as the Israelites were in the Old Testament and all the believers in the New Testament. It should be clear that for this spiritual priesthood no special clothing has been devised or deemed necessary. There is not a sound link that would justify that Eve, in a literal sense, was clothed as a priest.

Chapter 7

The Husband: Head or Caretaker?

"Unto the woman he said, I will greatly multiply thy sorrow and thy conception; in sorrow thou shalt bring forth children; and thy desire shall be to thy husband, and he shall rule over thee" (Gen. 3:16).

The Hebrew word *mashal* in the biblical phrase "and he shall rule over thee" clearly means: rule, have dominion, reign (Harris, *Theological Wordbook of the Old Testament*, p. 534). In Strong's *Exhaustive Concordance of the Bible*, we find the meaning of *mashal* in the Hebrew and Chaldee Dictionary, under number 4910: "to rule, (have, make to have) dominion, governor … reign, (bear, cause to, have) rule … have power."

Different translation. In order to pave the way for women's ordination, a team of learned men advocate that a more fitting and, therefore, preferable translation of the last phrase of Genesis 3:16 would be "and he will be responsible for you." This translation marks quite a change, but it is argued that this different translation agrees with an identical-looking but different Hebrew verb of *mashal* that means "to resemble or to be like," which would in this particular context, as is argued, emphasize the equality of Adam and Eve.

Accordingly, they state that there is no expression or sign of headship, hierarchy, or rulership, but only a blessing of responsible care taking and of equality. They refer to the fact that the man is to till the cursed ground of which is said that he would eat of it in sorrow (Gen. 2:5; 3:17). They explain that it appears that marriage in ancient times was based on man's provision of food, raiment, and marital duties (Exod. 21:10, 11).

Thus, they depict the man as a responsible provider and caretaker of his wife, which should be regarded as a blessing to her. Drawing on the meaning of the identical but different Hebrew verb of *mashal,* they argue that in a particular sense this verb could express the idea of responsibility, management, and caring. They explain that Eve was in need of care and should be served after her punishment of pain in childbirth. The particular function of the identical Hebrew verb of *mashal* in this context is regarded to balance her infliction of pain by the caring responsibility of her husband. But is the woman's balancing of her infliction of pain and sorrow not found in God's hopeful promise that is recorded in Genesis 3:15?

Furthermore, they point out that the idea of *ruling* would only be appropriate when someone of higher rank is involved, such as a king, leader, or master. Thus, in short, they try to justify their preferred translation above the common biblical version. To add more weight to their interpretation, they have constructed the following context pattern: The wife *supports* her husband, and the husband *clings* to his wife (Gen. 2:18, 24). The wife *longs* for her husband, and the husband *supports* his wife (Gen. 3:16). However, this pattern can only be constructed when the preferred interpretation of the last phrase of Genesis 3:16 is accepted.

Much stress is laid on the fact that men are made in God's image, so they are to show loving care to their wives. They argue that it is in harmony with God's character and actions, as revealed in the book of Genesis, where God presents Himself as a loving Father and Provider of all the needs of men and women. As we consider the viewpoint of care and responsibility, we certainly can accept the aspect of man's responsibility as a loving provider and caretaker for his wife and children. However, the comparison should not be made at the expense of God's delegated authority to men as head and ruler of the family.

Righteousness and judgment. God is indeed a loving Father and Provider of all human needs, but He is also a righteous Father: "Righteousness and judgment are the habitation of his throne" (Ps. 97:2). And so, on the one side, He shows mercy to thousands who love Him and keep His commandments, but on the other side, He visits with judgment the sins of those who are disobedient transgressors of His commandments.

Ellen White comments on this idea: "In all the Bible, God is represented not only as a tender father but as a righteous judge. Though He delights in showing mercy, and 'forgiving iniquity and transgression and sin,' yet He 'will by no means clear the guilty.' Exodus 34:7" (White, *Patriarchs and Prophets*, p. 469).

It is true that God's judgments, as long as Christ ministers in behalf of mankind, are always mingled with mercy and hope, but that does not belittle or eliminate a part of the judgment itself or turn it into some blessing. The sentence must, therefore, not be toned down but stand as it is, for to think that a loving, caring Father "will not be strict to punish their iniquity … is a fatal deception" (Ibid., p. 360).

The problem with the proposed translation and interpretation of the last part of Genesis 3:16 is that it eclipses some important, fundamental principles of God's pronounced sentence or law.

Normative sentence. As a result of sin, God pronounced a clear and normative sentence of man's authority over his wife and of woman's subjection and submission to her husband. This sentence fits its immediate context very well. God passed first sentence upon the serpent, for he had beguiled Eve (Gen. 3:14), and then he included a message of hope for fallen humanity (Gen. 3:15). "This sentence, uttered in the hearing of our first parents, was to them a promise" (White, *Patriarchs and Prophets*, pp. 65, 66).

After addressing the serpent, God proceeded to address the woman because she had transgressed His command. Note that God's sentence upon the woman was *preceded* by a promise of hope. However, as stated earlier, the hopeful message was not intended to derogate in any way the divine sentence of a righteous God. "Adam and Eve stood as criminals before the righteous Judge, awaiting the sentence which transgression had incurred; but before they heard of the life of toil and sorrow which must be their portion, or of the decree that they must return to dust, they listened to words that could not fail to give them hope. Though they must suffer from the power of their mighty foe, they could look forward to final victory" (Ibid., p. 66). Here we have a clear and lasting picture of the balance of pain and sorrow with hope and joy.

We are not to eclipse any part of the sentence or turn part of it somehow into a blessing, for the blessed promise of hope *preceded* the sentence. Thus, the argument that God is a loving Father and Provider of all human needs is demonstrated in the hopeful message given before the sentence was pronounced, while the sentence itself is a demonstration that God is a righteous

Judge. We cannot meddle with this and try to alleviate and belittle God's *sentence,* for this would tone down God's righteousness. God, being a caring and loving Father, fits the words of the promise of hope, while God, being a righteous Judge, fits the words of the sentence.

Unity and harmony by submission. If we take careful notice of Ellen White's explanation, it is perfectly clear that the last phrase of the sentence does not need to be changed or interpreted otherwise. The way we have it in our Bibles is very appropriate and in harmony with God's justice.

Ellen White comments: "And the Lord said, 'Thy desire shall be to thy husband, and he shall rule over thee.' In the creation God had made her the equal of Adam. Had they remained obedient to God—in harmony with His great law of love—they would ever have been in harmony with each other; but sin had brought discord, and now their union could be maintained and harmony preserved only by submission on the part of the one or the other. Eve had been the first in transgression; and she had fallen into temptation by separating from her companion, contrary to the divine direction. It was by her solicitation that Adam sinned, and she was now placed in subjection to her husband" (Ibid., p. 58).

Note how Ellen White quotes the last phrase of the divine sentence precisely as we have it in our Bibles: "and he shall rule over thee." Note how in harmony with this she explains that because sin brought discord, their union could be maintained and harmony preserved only by submission on the part of the one or the other and that Eve was now placed in subjection to her husband. This important truth would prevent much unnecessary grief, distress, and misery if taken to heart.

Emancipation. Many families are torn apart because there is no subjection, but emancipation, and each party follows the wishes of the heart. How important and relevant this biblical phrase of subjection is.

This is God's law, and if the principles enjoined in the divine law are practiced in the right way, it will result in harmony and happiness. Obedience to God's law, even if it concerns a sentence, is always profitable, while abuse will always result in misery.

Ellen White continued: "Had the principles joined in the law of God been cherished by the fallen race, this sentence, though growing out of the results of sin, would have proved a blessing to them; but man's abuse of the supremacy thus given him has too often rendered the lot of woman very bitter and made her life a burden" (Ibid., p. 58, 59).

It certainly is a serious mistake if we prefer to change God's law of life for humankind and eclipse the principle of subjection and submission of the woman to the man who is supposed to rule in a Christlike way for the benefit and happiness of the whole family.

Doing Abraham's works. Abraham "was called the Friend of God" and "the father of all them that believe" (James 2:23; Rom. 4:11). God knew him "that he will command his children and his household after him, and they shall keep the way of the Lord" (Gen. 18:19). Christ stressed that Abraham's children would do his works (John 8:39).

Note that Abraham was "ruler and priest of his own family, and he exerted authority over his children … His descendants were taught to look up to him as their head, in both religious and secular matters…. All were taught that they were under the rule of the God of heaven. There was to be no oppression on the part of parents and no disobedience on the part of children. God's law had appointed to each his duties, and only in obedience to it could any secure happiness or prosperity " (White, *Patriarchs and Prophets*, pp. 141, 142).

Should we do the works of Abraham or should we try to eliminate the principles of authority and government practiced by Abraham? If we do so are we not then upsetting the law of God? Note Ellen White's clear statement: "The Bible plainly states that the husband is the head of the family. 'Wives, submit yourselves unto your own husbands'" (White, *The Adventist Home*, p. 115).

Responsible position. Another quotation says: "The husband is the head of the family, as Christ is the head of the church, and any course which the wife may pursue to lessen his influence and lead him to come down from the dignified, responsible position God would have him occupy, displeases God. It is the duty of the wife to yield her wishes and will to her husband. Both should be yielding, but preference is given in the word of God to the judgment of the husband. And it will not detract from the dignity of the wife to yield to him whom she has chosen to be her counselor, adviser, and protector. The husband should maintain his position in his family with all meekness, yet with decision" (White, *Spiritual Gifts,* vol. 4b, p. 97).

Thus, it is clear that there is no equality. The husband is the head, and God desires that he occupy this dignified, responsible position. It is the duty of the wife to yield her wishes and will to him. This is clearly in harmony with God's law, pronounced to Eve: "and he shall rule over thee." These words may seem outdated in our modern time, but this is the way God ordained it. Remember that the man is the head of the family as Christ is the head of the church. Every husband should follow Christ's example. He should rule and exercise authority in a loving Christlike way just as Abraham did. In a loving, unselfish atmosphere, it will not be hard for a woman to submit her wishes and will to the guiding rule and authority of her loving husband.

Principle of authority. For a better understanding, it is important to note that in the earlier quoted *Theological Wordbook*, the use of the Hebrew word *mashal* (rule) is compared in different contexts: "Eve, standing for all wives, was given to understand that in the home the husband 'shall rule over thee' (Gen 3:16). Such leadership as is appropriate—and it varies greatly—for a man to give his family is meant. Cain was told by God that he ought to master sin in his life. 'Do thou rule over him' (Gen 4:7). Management over all the material goods of a master, as his steward, and management of all the personnel of the enterprise is indicated in the case of Abraham's 'servant … his eldest servant of his house, that ruled over all that he had' (Gen 24:2). Direction of affairs of a large family as 'firstborn-designate' is indicated by Joseph's version of the sheaves—at least so his angry brothers interpreted his vision: 'Shalt thou indeed reign over us' (Gen 37:8). *Mashal* is used of Joseph's administration of Egypt as Pharaoh's prime minister. So Joseph claimed he had been made 'a ruler throughout all the land of Egypt' (Gen 45:8); and his brothers agreed, 'he is governor over all the land of Egypt' (Gen 45:26)" (Harris, *Theological Wordbook of the Old Testament*, p. 534).

At the end of the different comparative uses of the word *mashal*, we read the following important conclusion: "There is no specific theology to be drawn from the meaning of the word. Yet the passages cited and the seventy or so others not cited demonstrate the importance of the principle of authority, the absolute moral necessity of respect for proper authority, the value of it for orderly society and happy living and the origin of all authority in God, himself. Authority is of many degrees and kinds. It has various theoretical bases. It originates in God. Man has no authority at all as man but simply as God's vice regent" (Ibid).

Conclusion. Thus, we can conclude that the phrase in Genesis 3:16, "and he shall rule over thee," implies that God has entrusted *authority* to the husband over his wife.

Note that the use of the word *mashal* in the different passages of the Bible demonstrate the importance of the principle of authority. This important principle, however, is eclipsed and replaced by the principle of caring or supporting as we accept the proposed translation: "and he will be responsible for you." We just cannot go along with this interpretation, for it changes and undermines God's law by which *authority* is delegated to the man as God's vice regent. This delegated authority by divine law addressed to the woman should, by no means, be yielded. Ellen White wrote, "The father must not betray his sacred trust. He must not, on any point, yield up his parental authority" (White, *The Adventist Home*, p. 212).

It is a most serious thing when we tarnish God's righteousness and eclipse important principles, such as authority, subjection, and submission, of God's law of life proclaimed by God himself to fallen humanity. We should not try to change or adapt this divine law according to our own preferred understanding and interpretation. God will not hold those guiltless who do so.

Chapter 8

The Biblical Principle of the Priesthood of all Believers

Does the New Testament principle of the "priesthood of all believers" somehow justify that women, equivalent with men, are called to positions of authority and leadership in the church? Let us consider how this principle works out.

The apostle Peter states in his first letter: "Unto you therefore which believe he is precious ... ye are a chosen generation, a royal priesthood, a holy nation, a peculiar people" (1 Peter 2:7, 9). Here the apostle repeats the words that were spoken to the Israelites when they were led out of Egypt and had pitched their tents at Sinai. We read: "Now therefore, if ye will obey my voice indeed, and keep my covenant, then ye shall be a peculiar treasure unto me ... and ye shall be unto me a kingdom of priests, and a holy nation" (Exod. 19:5, 6).

God promised that the Israelites would be a "kingdom of priests." In ancient times not everyone was, in the literal sense, a priest who offered animal sacrifices unto the Lord. Only the head of the family or tribe usually assumed this priestly role.

When Israel was organized as a nation, the tribe of Levi was chosen to serve in the tabernacle in place of the firstborn or head of each family. The tribe of Levi remained loyal to God when the golden calf was worshiped and the Levites were now chosen to serve the Lord. Aaron and his sons were set apart for the priestly office.

Although the whole nation was called a "kingdom of priests," this promise clearly could not mean that every Israelite was to be a priest serving in the tabernacle or temple. Only the sons of Aaron of the tribe of Levi were, according to the law, allowed to minister in the Lord's house as priests (see Heb. 7:11–14). There is no reason to believe, nor any indication to suggest, that others or any woman was ever called to serve as such in the house of the Lord.

A Spiritual priesthood. But it was not only the tribe of Levi that was called a "kingdom of priests." These words were addressed to all Israelites. Since the priesthood was reserved only for the Levitical male offspring of Aaron's house, the phrase "kingdom of priests" must have another meaning that applies to all Israelites, male or female, for the entire congregation was included in the plan of God. In what sense then, were all Israelites called to be a "kingdom of priests"?

The previous verse, Exodus 19:4, says: "Ye have seen what I did unto the Egyptians, and how I bare you on eagles' wings, and brought you unto myself." The Israelites had been in Egypt in a state of servitude and bondage, and they were now, according to God's promise, to be gathered and built into a kingdom, a free state governed by the laws that God would give them. They were to be a kingdom unto God, a theocracy with God as their King. God purposed that this kingdom would consist of people who were priests, devoted to the worship and service of God. They were to be people who had access to God, served Him, offered sacrifices to Him, obeyed His voice, and kept His covenant. By faith in the promised Messiah, they were to enter God's kingdom of grace and gain victory over sin, over Satan, and over the world. They were, as a peculiar treasure, as a kingdom of priests, and as a holy and separate nation (Exod. 19:5, 6), to draw nigh to God to present themselves, souls and bodies, a holy and living sacrifice and offer to God the sacrifices of prayer and praise. Such was the elevated priestly calling of the Israelites (cf. White, *Patriarchs and Prophets*, p. 352; Rom. 12:1). God had chosen them to reflect His character and be the light of the world. They were to be priests in a spiritual sense.

The kingdom given to the Gentiles who would share the same blessing. If the Israelites had obeyed these divine instructions, they would have been the world's object lesson of health and prosperity. The Israelites, however, failed to fulfill God's purpose, and thus failed to receive the rich blessings that might have been theirs. Instead, they fulfilled a darker promise: "The kingdom of God shall be taken from you, and given to a nation bringing forth the fruits thereof"

(Matt. 21:43). From the olive tree, as a presentation of the house of Israel, branches were broken off and believing Gentiles were grafted in their place and made to share the root and richness of the olive tree (Rom. 11:17). Could this mean that the Gentiles were made to share other blessings than the Israelites were to receive? Is there any difference? No, the Gentiles, through faith, were made to share the same root with the same richness. They were blessed with faithful Abraham and not blessed *apart* from Abraham with *another* blessing: "Know ye therefore that they which are of faith, the same are the children of Abraham ... so then they which be of faith are blessed with faithful Abraham" (Gal. 3:7, 9).

Thus the apostle Peter repeats the same priestly calling and applies it to the New Testament believers: "Ye are a chosen generation, a royal priesthood, a holy nation, a peculiar people" (1 Peter 2:9). Does this mean that all believers are to be priests in a literal sense? That has never been God's order. In Old Testament times only the Levites ministered in the house of the Lord and they were sustained by the tithes of the other tribes. In a similar sense, in New Testament times the ministers of the Gospel were to be sustained by the tithes of other believers who were not called to be ministers in God's church (1 Cor. 9:13, 14).

Christ, our great High Priest, lives forever, and has "an unchangeable priesthood" (Heb. 7:24). Goodspeed uses the word "untransferable." Weymouth's translation says: "which does not pass to any successor." Charles B. Williams' *A Translation in the Language of the People*, words Hebrews 7:24 as follows: "[He] enjoys the only priesthood that has no successors in office." Thus it is clear that there is *no* place for a literal human priesthood in New Testament times.

Spiritual kings and priests. The application of the phrase "a royal priesthood" to all believers cannot be taken literally. In the Old Testament, the whole congregation of Israel was called "a kingdom of priests" and similarly, in the New Testament, the whole congregation of believers is called 'a royal priesthood.' Thus the same principle, with the same meaning, applies in the New Testament.

The Israelites were called out of Egypt's servitude and bondage into God's royal kingdom of grace, to reveal His character to other nations. The New Testament believers are similarly called out of the world from the servitude and bondage of sin and set free in God's kingdom. Cleansed by Christ's blood, they are kings and priests with the right to all its privileges, since God's kingdom of grace is set up within the obedient and faithful believer. Through the priestly ministry of Christ, they are anointed with the Holy Spirit and sanctified by His grace.

Spiritual sacrifices. As spiritual priests they offer the sacrifice of a broken heart and contrite spirit (Ps. 51:17), presenting their bodies a living sacrifice (Rom. 12:1). They come near to God and offer their spiritual sacrifices of prayer and praise. Grace is the reigning principle implanted in their lives and revealed in righteousness, true holiness, peace and joy. They have the power of kings over sin, Satan, and the world. They reveal the graceful riches of kings in this life and are entitled to receive the riches of glory in the life to come. They live like kings, wearing the royal robe of Christ's righteousness. They sit at the King's table and eat from the bread of life and are attended on as kings by angels as their lifeguards and ministering spirits. And as heirs of God's kingdom of glory, they will sit with Christ on His throne and reign with Him as kings and priests.

Ambassadors for Christ with different roles. Since the atoning death of Christ there are no priests to offer sacrifices in the temple. And since there is but one heavenly Mediator between God and man, there is no need of a human priest serving as such. However, the word and ministry of reconciliation has been committed to all believers, and they are, as ambassadors for Christ, to beseech people to be reconciled to God (2 Cor. 5:18–20).

All true believers are part of the royal priesthood to shew forth the praises of Him Who called them into His marvellous light (1 Peter 2:9). They are all to proclaim God´s character, His abounding love and gracious plan of salvation. All believers, men and women, are ambassadors for Christ, called to proclaim His everlasting gospel of salvation. Are we to understand, then, that this commission from God indicates the complete functional equality of men and women?

As previously noted, bishops and elders are Christ's ambassadors in a special sense, by virtue of their office. In the church different roles apply to men and women (1 Tim. 2:8–15; 1 Tim. 3:1–5; Titus 1:5–9), while the father still retains the priestly aspect of the household. Ellen White says: "In a sense the father is the priest of the household, laying upon the family altar the morning and evening sacrifice. But the wife and children should unite in prayer and join in the song of praise" (White, *My Life Today*, p. 203).

A living relation with God. The expression "a royal priesthood, a holy nation, a peculiar people" indicates that there are faithful believers who have a living relationship with God that will result in a life of victory over sin and reveal the character of Christ, who is their Priest and King. The victorious lives of such dedicated, faithful men and women will be a most powerful witness to the world, and that is what the apostle Peter aimed at in calling the believers "a royal priesthood, a holy nation, a peculiar people."

Ellen White explains: "The early Christians were indeed a peculiar people. Their blameless deportment and unswerving faith were a continual reproof that disturbed the sinner's peace. Though few in numbers, without wealth, position, or honorary titles, they were a terror to evildoers wherever their character and doctrines were known" (White, *The Great Controversy*, p. 46).

The main theme of the gospel. Reflecting Christ's character is the main theme of the Gospel for every faithful believer. Note Ellen White's words: "Christ is waiting with longing desire for the manifestation of Himself in His church. When the character of Christ shall be perfectly reproduced in His people, then He will come to claim them as His own" (White, *Christ's Object Lessons*, p. 69). Calling the believers "a royal priesthood, a holy nation, a peculiar people," succinctly expresses this supreme purpose of reproducing Christ's character in His people.

Peter does not focus on offices in the church. Peter refers to God's church on earth, when he states: "Ye also, as lively stones, are built up a spiritual house, a holy priesthood, to offer up spiritual sacrifices, acceptable to God by Jesus Christ" (1 Peter 2:5). It should be clear, however, that Peter is not speaking about offices in the church, and therefore, he does not focus on the requirements for occupying a responsible position of leadership and authority in the church. On the contrary, he speaks here of a personal, living relationship with God that results in offering up spiritual sacrifices and reflecting His character. To conclude, then, that the biblical principle of the priesthood of all believers, as presented by Peter, justifies that women could be chosen to occupy responsible positions of leadership and authority in the church, is therefore, in this context, without biblical support.

No change. There is no contradiction on this point among the Bible writers. They were all inspired by the Holy Spirit, and Paul, speaking about order in the church, clearly testifies: "The things that I write unto you are the commandments of the Lord" (1 Cor. 14:37). Thus we should not doubt that the counsel he presented was a clear word from the Lord and not a reflection of his own ideas. Indeed, we should take Paul's teaching most seriously and remember that the inspired apostle communicated divine wisdom applying it "at all times, in all places, and under all conditions" (White, *The Acts of the Apostles*, p. 303).

Human beings may change their attitude, views, and ideas, but the Lord God never changes (Mal. 3:6). There "is no variableness, neither shadow of turning" with our heavenly Father (James 1:17). He testifies: I will not "alter the thing that has gone out of my lips" (Ps. 89:34). And Jesus Christ is: "the same yesterday, and to day, and for ever" (Heb. 13:8).

Thus, if Paul wrote the word of God, as we all firmly believe, then we can be absolutely sure that Paul's inspired teachings are just as true in this modern age as they were in his days. Therefore, we should not meddle in any way with the clear words of instruction he wrote in all his epistles to the various churches.

Diverse rights and relations. Ellen White wrote: "The Scriptures are plain upon the relations and rights of men and women" (White, *Testimonies for the Church*, vol. 1, p. 421). Note, she did not write: the relations and rights of *humanity*; she clearly specified *men* and *women*. Thus the Bible does not equalize men and women, but presents their different rights and relations. In relation to each other, the Bible clearly points out the differences in their roles. The man was formed first and he was not created for the woman, but the woman was created for the man. She was made from the rib of the man as a helpmate for him. Although he capitulated later to temptation by Eve, the man was not deceived first; the woman was. After the fall, God said unto the woman that her desire shall be to her husband and he shall rule over her. Wives should submit themselves unto their own husbands. The husband is the head of the wife. Wives should be in subjection to their husbands. As the church is subject unto Christ, so wives should be to their husbands in everything. Husbands should love their wives and wives should reverence their husbands. Sara, for example, obeyed Abraham and called him master (Gen. 2:20, 3:16; 1 Cor. 11:3, 7, 8; Eph. 5:22, 23, 24, 33; Col. 3:18; 1 Tim. 2:11, 13, 14; 1 Peter 3:1, 4–6). Although these ideas may not be in harmony with modern cultural practices, shouldn't we, as committed Christians, revere these Bible texts equally with the other inspired parts of God's sure and abiding word? These passages are clearly in line with the law of life, pronounced as a sentence upon Eve, whereby the principle of authority is delegated to the man as the head and ruler of the family, while the principle of subjection and submission is required of the woman.

Christ's example. It is important to notice that Christ chose only men as apostles—no women were chosen. The church has followed this example for about two thousand years. If, indeed, it is in harmony with God's word that women should also be apostles or priests, then Christ and the apostles were wrong in not appointing a female apostle at the formation of the church.

The early church was equally open to Jewish and Gentile believers—although a firm stand was taken on matters such as circumcision and other requirements of the Jewish law—so why not women leaders? Some people argue that Christ and the apostles were bound by the rules, customs, and culture of their age. They explain that if the atmosphere in the ancient world would have been more accepting of women we would certainly have witnessed the ordination of women leaders in the church. Is this really a good argument in favor of women's ordination?

Kallistos Ware aptly explained: "Jesus Christ is not only complete man but true and perfect God. He is within history, but also above history. We do not see in him merely a human teacher, bound by the conventions of his age; he is the Word of God, from whose lips we hear not private opinions soon to grow outdated, but the eternal truth. Indeed, far from being subservient to contemporary customs, Christ often showed a striking independence. He told his disciples, 'You have heard what was said by the men of old; but I say to you…' (Matt. 5.21-2); he claimed to be master of the Sabbath, openly breaking the accepted regulations; he ate with tax-collectors and sinners; to the astonishment of his followers he spoke with a Samaritan woman, and in general ignored rules normally observed by a Jewish rabbi of the time in his dealings with the female sex. Thus if the Son of God had wanted to appoint women as apostles, he would have done so, whatever the existing conventions within Judaism or elsewhere in the ancient world. And the fact that he did *not* choose them as apostles must remain decisive for us today. Are we to assert that the incarnate Word and Wisdom of God was mistaken, and that we at the end of the twentieth century understand the truth better than he did?" (Moore, *Man, Woman, and Priesthood*, p. 73).

Thus, because Christ did not call women to the apostolic ministry, we should regard the matter as definitive and definite, for there is perfect harmony in the Bible and Jesus' practices while on the earth. Furthermore, Christ's example is in line with the pronounced sentence upon Eve. As our guide, His example is still valid to follow. He recognized and honored the place of women in the home, the church, and society, but He did not call them to be apostles, priests, or other church leaders.

The New Testament Church is "built upon the foundation of the apostles and prophets, Jesus Christ himself being the chief corner stone" (Eph. 2:20). Does the foundation of the church also include women? As we look at the structure of the New Jerusalem do we then find the name of a woman written thereon? Although several dedicated, reputable women are mentioned in the Bible, not even one of them is named. The twelve gates and twelve foundations have only male names written on them: the twelve apostles and the sons of Jacob or the twelve tribes of Israel (Rev. 21:12-14). This, certainly, is not just by chance but according to God's plan and providence and clearly in line with the teaching of the whole Bible.

Slavery. Other people argue that, similar to the issue of slavery, the church has realized that women should have an equal place with men in the church and be ordained and given the same responsibilities as men. They present the theory that the apostles did not immediately raise their hands against the evils of slavery; instead, it took a long time for the church to abandon slavery and speak out against it. They postulate that it has also taken a long time for the church to realize that men and women are equally qualified to assume a leading role in the church and be ordained.

As we consider this argument, however, we should note that there is no sound parallel between the ordination of women and the evils of slavery. Oppression and slavery were often a divine punishment for continued disobedience. However, the concept of slavery in the Bible differs greatly with the practiced excesses of slavery in later ages. Slaves in the context of the Bible had human rights with social privileges (Exod. 12:43, 44; 21:1-11, 26, 27; Deut. 15:12-18; 23:15, 16). Their position was more like a servant. The frequently used Greek word *doulos* in the New Testament means "slave, servant."

Furthermore, we should note that it is not true that the apostles did not raise their hands against the evil forms of slavery. Paul, for instance, "taught principles which struck at the very foundation of slavery and which, if carried into effect, would surely undermine the whole system" (White, *The Acts of the Apostles*, pp. 459, 460). It should be clear, therefore, that there is no sound bearing on the connection between slavery and the position of women in the church, since there is too much difference in this comparison.

Chapter 9

Not a Teacher

The apostle Paul is very clear on the position of a woman. As an authoritative apostle of Jesus Christ, he plainly declared: "But I suffer not a woman to teach, nor to usurp authority over the man, but to be in silence. For Adam was first formed, then Eve" (1 Tim. 2:12). Why is a woman not allowed to teach? Is something wrong when a woman is engaged as a teacher? What does the apostle Paul precisely mean and how are we to understand this statement?

The Greek word for "teacher" is *didaskalos*—from *didaskoo*, to teach. In the Bible, a *didaskalos* is also frequently rendered "Master," and in the Gospels this word is used to address Christ (Matt. 8:19, 17:24, 26:18; Mark 4:38, 5:35, 14:14; Luke 8:49, 22:11; John 11:28, etc.) In John 1:38 it replaces "rabbi" and in John 20:16, it replaces "rabboni." In John 3:10 it is used to address Nicodemus, the master (teacher) of Israel. In Luke 2:46 it designates the "doctors" (teachers) in the temple.

Didaskalos corresponds to the title *rabbei*, "an Aramaic word signifying 'my master,' a title of respectful address to Jewish teachers." The word "'epistates' denotes a chief, a commander, overseer, master … The form 'epistata'… alongside of the commoner 'didaskale' is … a Greek synonym for the latter, and both are to be traced back to the Aramaic 'rabbei'" (Vine, *The Expanded Vine's Expository Dictionary of New Testament Words*, pp. 729, 925). "'Didaskalos' corresponds to the title 'rabbi' and is used as a title of respect. It is used of John the Baptist (Luke 3:12), of Jewish learned men (Luke 2:46, John 3:10), of an official of the Christian church. Acts 13:1; 1 Corinthians 12:28f; Ephesians 4:11; 2 Timothy 1:11; James 3:1" (Arndt, *A Greek-English Lexicon of the New Testament*, p. 190).

Another source states that *didaskalos* is used (among others) "of the teachers of the Jewish religion; of those who by their great power as teachers drew crowds about them; of the apostles; of Paul, (1 Timothy 2:7; 2 Timothy 1:11); of those who in the religious assemblies of Christians undertook the work of teaching, with the special assistance of the Holy Spirit. 1 Corinthians 12:28 sq.; Ephesians 4:11; Acts 13:1; cf. James 3:1" (Thayer, *A Greek-English Lexicon of the New Testament, being Grimm's Wilke's Clavis Novi Testamenti*, p. 144).

Thus, the office of a teacher connotes influence, dignity, authority and leadership. A teacher was regarded as a chief and master and addressed as rabbi. Paul makes it clear that a woman should not occupy such a position in the church. She should not usurp or exercise authority. Her divinely appointed work is, in the first place, to care for her family and to teach and educate her children in the ways of the Lord. "But if a woman does not care for those of hers, even those of her own house, then she has denied her faith and she is worse than an unbeliever" (1 Tim. 5:8, Dutch NV translation). In the Bible, the position and chief duty of a woman is thus clearly indicated.

> Paul indicates that certain specified officers are expected to exercise the function of teaching the congregation. He here is urging women to be careful neither to interrupt the worship nor to assume the place of public official teachers in the Christian Church … Paul does not mean that a woman is mentally or morally or spiritually inferior to a man. Both men and women have the defects of their qualities. However, both are on the same plane before God and are heirs to his eternal salvation. Therefore, Paul adds that, while a woman need not assume the official duties of a Christian pastor, nevertheless she may enjoy all the benefits of salvation, in her own more natural sphere of wife and mother, if she continues to be faithful and loving and holy, as well as modest and womanly in her demeanor … If he [Paul] does, however, in passages like this, distinguish between the respective duties of men and of women, it appears to many that this distinction 'lies deep down in the facts of human nature as originally constituted.' (Erdman, *The Pastoral Epistles of Paul*, pp. 35, 36)

Although the service of women in the time of Christ and in the apostolic church was very valuable and much appreciated, we do not find evidence that they were called to occupy offices of leadership and authority in the church. In line with this, women are welcome to teach; however, teaching in the position of being a ruling leader, like a rabbi, will be out of harmony with Paul's direction.

With reference to the law, Creation, and the fall, Paul made it clear that, by divine appointment, the chief duty of a woman is to be a good and faithful mother. She should not rule the church, but should recognize that God has given the responsibility of leadership to man. This principle applies as much today as in the days of the apostles. God is not changed and what has gone out of His mouth will not be altered. Notwithstanding cultural differences, all Christians in all places of this world can safely rely on this sure biblical foundation and build their faith and insight harmoniously upon it and act accordingly.

Chapter 10

Leaders in the Church

The apostles, realizing the solemn and heavy impact of ruling God's church, chose able men with a good reputation for responsible positions of leadership. They followed the divine instructions carefully.

> Solemn are the responsibilities resting upon those who are called to act as leaders in the church of God on earth. In the days of the theocracy, when Moses was endeavoring to carry alone burdens so heavy that he would soon have worn away … was counseled by Jethro … that men be appointed to act as 'rulers …' These were to be 'able men, such as fear God, men of truth, hating covetousness.'… In harmony with this plan, 'Moses chose able men out of all Israel, and made them heads over the people, rulers … And they judged the people at all seasons. (White, *The Acts of the Apostles*, pp. 92–94; see also Exod. 18:19–26)

> Later, when choosing seventy elders to share with him the responsibilities of leadership, Moses was careful to select, as his helpers, men possessing dignity, sound judgment, and experience. In his charge to these elders at the time of their ordination, he outlined some of the qualifications that fit a man to be a wise ruler in the church. (White, *The Acts of the Apostles*, p. 94; see also Deut. 1:16, 17)

> King David, toward the close of his reign, delivered a solemn charge to those bearing the burden of the work of God in his day.

> Summoning to Jerusalem 'all the princes of Israel, the princes of the tribes, and the captains… and the stewards… with the officers, and with the mighty men, and with all the valiant men,' the aged king solemnly charged them, 'in the sight of all Israel the congregation of the Lord, and in the audience of our God,' to 'keep and seek for all the commandments of the Lord your God.' (White, *The Acts of the Apostles*, p. 94; see also 1 Chron. 28:1, 8)

It is clear that in Old Testament times only able men were chosen for positions of leadership and authority. In accordance with God's unchanging rule, the same principles apply in New Testament times:

> The same principles of piety and justice that were to guide the rulers among God's people in the time of Moses and of David, were also to be followed by those given the oversight of the newly organized church of God in the gospel dispensation. In the work of setting things in order in all the churches, and ordaining suitable men to act as officers, the apostles held to the high standards of leadership outlined in the Old Testament Scriptures. They maintained that he who is called to stand in a position of leading responsibility in the church 'must be blameless holding fast the faithful word as he hath been taught, that he may be able by sound doctrine both to exhort and to convince the gainsayers.' (White, *The Acts of the Apostles*, p. 95; see also Titus 1:7–9)

Thus, according to God's inspired word and Ellen White's writings, suitable men were ordained. The Old Testament standards of leadership were maintained. Accordingly, there is not one clear example in the Bible of a woman priest, apostle, elder, presbyter, overseer, or bishop. If there is no hint nor reference in this direction, would it be advisable to go beyond the biblical instructions and ordain women in such offices of leadership? Would it not be preferable to stay within the limit of biblical rule and agree that in the unfailing providence of God, this issue has already been settled?

Chapter 11

A Solemn Responsibility

A very important and solemn responsibility of a church leader is to reprove sin. Note Ellen White's words:

> Those whom God has set apart as ministers of righteousness have solemn responsibilities laid upon them to reprove the sins of the people. Paul commanded Titus: 'These things speak, and exhort, and rebuke with all authority. Let no man despise thee.' There are ever those who will despise the one who dares to reprove sin; but there are times when reproof must be given. Paul directs Titus to rebuke a certain class sharply, that they may be sound in the faith. Men and women who, with their different organizations, are brought together in church capacity have peculiarities and faults. As these are developed, they will require reproof. If those who are placed in important positions never reproved, never rebuked, there would soon be a demoralized condition of things that would greatly dishonor God. (White, *Testimonies for the Church*, vol. 3, p. 358)

Note further how sad it is when ministers fail to rebuke sin: "To neglect this duty, or to be slothful and careless in its performance, is to disobey God, to sanction sin, and to bring his wrath upon his people" (White, *Signs of the Times*, December 8, 1881, p. 541).

Will this solemn responsibility of reproving sin be an easy task to perform? It is very true that some will despise the one who dares to reprove their sins. The pastor who faithfully preaches God's word, thereby condemning the sins of the people, too often incurs their hatred, but this solemn work must be done. It is an essential part of a minister's work, which will, if neglected, bring about God's displeasure and wrath. A minister who fails to rebuke sin, will be a curse, like Israel's high priest Eli, whose unfaithfulness "gave rise to a long train of evils, bringing crime and anguish upon a whole nation" (Ibid.).

Thus, nobody needs to doubt the importance and seriousness of this essential part of a minister's work, which should never be neglected but always faithfully performed. A revival and reformation is urgent. Sins that cause separation must be sternly rebuked and confessed. Ellen White writes: "Today there is need of the voice of stern rebuke; for grievous sins have separated the people from God" (White, *Prophets and Kings*, p. 140).

Now what if a woman who was in authority had to perform this solemn duty of reproving sin? What if a woman had to rebuke a man? If a woman were ordained as a responsible leader or pastor in the church, then this essential duty of reproving sin would inevitably be a solemn part of her responsibility. She would have to impartially rebuke the sins of the members of the church. She would have to rebuke men also.

Is it the will of God that a woman should carry the authoritative burden of rebuking a man, or would this be against God's order? No one likes to be reproved. Reproof often evokes resentment. Would men accept reproof given by a woman? If a man should need stern rebuke, would he accept it from a woman? If this is a hard duty and responsibility for a male minister to perform, how much more difficult for a woman in authority? Would it be possible that such action on the part of a woman minister could undermine a good understanding and create problems in the church, more than when a man reproves sin?

Is it any wonder that Paul writes by divine inspiration that a woman should not usurp or exercise authority over the man? Is it any wonder that in the all-wise order of God a woman is not called to occupy a leading position of solemn responsibility and authority in the church? What then is precisely the function and ministry of women in the church?

Chapter 12

Ministry of Women

The apostle Paul, after having listed the necessary qualifications of a leader or bishop in the church, proceeds to list those of deacons (1 Tim. 3:8–13). In verse 11 we read: "The women likewise must be serious, no slanderers, but temperate, faithful in all things" (RSV). *The Twentieth Century, New Testament, A Translation into Modern English* says: "It should be the same with women. They should be serious, not gossips, sober, and trustworthy in all respects." If we compare different translations on this text, we notice that several use the word "women," some use "wives," while a few others use the word "deaconesses," such as *The Centenary Translation* by H. B. Montgomery and *The New Testament: A Translation in the Language of the People* by Charles B. Williams. The *Expositor's Greek Testament*, edited by W. Robertson Nicoll, explains: "These are the deaconesses, ministrae (Pliny, Ep. X. 97.) of whom Phoebe (Rom. xvi. 1) is an undoubted example. They performed for the women of the early church the same sort of ministrations that the deacons did for the men" (p. 115). J. A. Bengel states: "The meaning is women deacons, deaconesses" (Bengel, *New Testament Word Studies*, p. 519).

Some Bible translations have the word "their" added, which is not in the Greek and would interpret the women as the wives of the deacons. *The Translator's New Testament* has the note: "There is no word for 'their' in the Greek text here; the Greek word 'gunē' means either 'wife' or 'woman', and it is not certain which is intended here. If it is 'woman,' the reference will be to women church workers or 'deaconesses,' parallel to the deacons in the same paragraph" (Bradnock, p. 515).

Since the word "their" is not in the Greek and since we know that women were active as deaconesses in the apostolic church, we may well regard this Bible passage as referring to deaconesses. They can do a special work that is not fitted for men. Thus, there is no perfect equality. Ellen White makes clear that in some respects a different role applies to men and women because some tasks are more womanlike and not very appropriate for men to accomplish. The reverse is also true as is denoted in some of the quotes featured under the following headings.

A work not appointed to men. Ellen White states that deaconesses have a work in the church not appointed to men. Writing to a conference president, she urged:

> You are not to set such an example that women will feel at liberty to tell you the grievances of their home life, and to draw upon your sympathies. When a woman comes to you with her troubles, tell her plainly to go to her sisters, to tell her troubles to the deaconesses of the church. Tell her that she is out of place in opening her troubles to any man, for men are easily beguiled and tempted. Tell the one who has thrown her case upon you that God has not placed this burden upon any man. You are not wise to take these burdens upon yourself. It is not your appointed work. (White, *Manuscript Release*, vol. 21, pp. 97, 98)

Laboring in the gospel ministry; visiting the flock. "There are women who should labor in the gospel ministry. In many respects they would do more good than the ministers who neglect to visit the flock of God" (White, *Manuscript Releases,* vol. 5, pp. 325, 326).

Equality with men in several respects. "Woman, if she wisely improves her time and her faculties, relying upon God for wisdom and strength, may stand on an equality with her husband as adviser, counselor, companion, and co-worker, and yet lose none of her womanly grace or modesty. She may elevate her own character, and just as she does this she is elevating and ennobling the characters of her family, and exerting a powerful though unconscious influence upon others around her" (White, *Good Health*, June 1880).

Women's ministry is greatly needed. "We greatly need consecrated women who, as messengers of mercy, shall visit the mothers and the children in their homes, and help them in the every-day household duties, if need be, before beginning to talk to them regarding the truth for this time. You will find that by this method you will have souls as the result of your ministry" (White, *Review and Herald*, July 12, 1906).

Home missionary work for women that men cannot do. "The Lord has a work for women as well as for men ... The Saviour will reflect upon these self-sacrificing women the light of His countenance, and will give them a power that exceeds that of men. They can do in families a work that men cannot do, a work that reaches the inner life. They can come close to the hearts of those whom men cannot reach. Their labor is needed" (White, *Review and Herald*, August 26, 1902).

Women were helping Christ and labored with Paul. "Christ speaks of women who helped Him in presenting the truth before others, and Paul also speaks of women who labored with him in the gospel. But how very limited is the work done by those who could do a large work if they would" (White, *The Review and Herald*, July 21, 1896).

A wide field of service for women. "In the various branches of the work of God's cause, there is a wide field in which our sisters may do good service for the Master. Many lines of missionary work are neglected ... Through various lines of home missionary effort they can reach a class that is not reached by our ministers. Among the noble women who have had the moral courage to decide in favor of the truth for this time are many who have tact, perception, and good ability, and who may make successful workers. The labors of such Christian women are needed" (White, *Review and Herald*, December 10, 1914).

Holding Bible classes. "Intelligent women, if truly converted, can act a part in this work of holding Bible classes. There is a wide field of service for women as well as for men" (White, Letter 84, 1910).

Successful Bible instructors. "There are women who are especially adapted for the work of giving Bible readings, and they are very successful in presenting the Word of God in its simplicity to others. They become a great blessing in reaching mothers and their daughters. This is a sacred work, and those engaged in it should receive encouragement" (White, Letter 108, 1910).

Addressing the congregation when ministers are away. "Sister R and Sister W are doing just as efficient work as the ministers; and some meetings when the ministers are all called away, Sister W takes the Bible and addresses the congregation" (White, Letter 169, 1900).

The refining softening influence of women is needed in preaching the truth. "Women can be the instruments of righteousness, rendering holy service. It was Mary that first preached a risen Jesus ... The refining, softening influence of Christian women is needed in the great work of preaching the truth" (White, *Review and Herald*, January 2, 1879).

God's helping hands. "Wake up, wake up, my brethren and sisters. You must do the work that Christ did when He was upon this earth. Remember that you may act as God's helping hand in opening the prison doors to those that are bound. Wonderful is the work that God desires to accomplish through His servants, that His name may constantly be glorified. He is waiting to work through His people. Those who are willing to be used will obtain a rich experience, an experience of the goodness of God. Of those who act as His helping hand the Lord says, 'Ye shall be named the Priests of the Lord; men shall call you the ministers of our God'" (White, *Manuscript Releases*, vol. 16, p. 75).

Some people have made much of this passage, explaining that Ellen White is addressing brethren and sisters alike to act as God's helping hand, and since she quotes Isaiah 61:6, they fervently point out that men and women are equally named the priests of the Lord and called to be ministers of our God. Thus, they conclude that women are, just as men, called to the priesthood and, as such, may be equally ordained as ministers of the gospel.

It should be noticed, however, that the quoted Bible text does not say, "Ye shall be the Priests of the Lord"; instead, it clearly says, "Ye shall be *named* the Priests of the Lord." To *be* a priest and be *named* a priest is not necessarily the same—there is a difference. In Hebrew the word for priests is *kohen*. This word is widely used in a *specific* sense to describe the literal priests who officiated in the temple, but it is also used in a *general* sense to describe the spiritual priesthood in Exodus 19:6: "And ye shall be unto me a kingdom of priests" (*kohen*). We must admit that in this general sense every faithful believer is part of that kingdom and named a priest, men and women alike. However, if we study Isaiah 61:6 in its context, it is clear that the verse is not referring to the officiating priesthood in the temple but that it is pointing to the spiritual priesthood. With this determination, it should be noted that this priesthood does not include ordination for all believers. There is no evidence nor indication that this kind of priesthood has ever fitted out the church with functional gender equality and so there is in this context no reason to suggest women ordination.

Many Bible commentators refer to the spiritual priesthood. Joseph Benson comments on Isaiah 61:6: "The whole body of you shall now be as near to God as the priests were formerly, and shall be a royal priesthood, 1 Peter 2:9. This is most certainly true of all the faithful under the gospel" (Benson, *The Holy Bible Containing the Old and New Testaments: With Critical, Explanatory, and Practical Notes,* vol. III, p. 2717).

To be part of God's spiritual kingdom and spiritual priesthood is not a permit or license for women to be ordained to the gospel ministry.

Set apart by prayer and laying on of hands. "Women who are willing to consecrate some of their time to the service of the Lord should be appointed to visit the sick, look after the young, and minister to the necessities of the poor. They should be set apart to this work by prayer and laying on of hands. In some cases they will need to counsel with the church officers or the minister; but if they are devoted women, maintaining a vital connection with God, they will be a power for good in the church" (White, *Review and Herald,* July 9, 1895).

Note that in this last quotation women are not set apart or ordained as leaders in the church with full ecclesiastical authority. The context makes clear that they are set apart to serve the church in capacities befitting a woman, such as the work of deaconesses.

Although we are not able to find any support that a woman could be ordained and occupy a responsible, leading position in the church with full ecclesiastical authority, it is clear that the Bible and Ellen White value women's work highly. Ellen White emphasizes repeatedly that there is a great and important work to be done by women in the church, and that they should be set apart for their special work by prayer and laying on of hands. If this "laying on of hands" is not an ordination, how are we then to understand this act?

Chapter 13

Ordination vs. the Laying on of Hands

In both the Old and New Testaments various Hebrew and Greek verbs are used for "to set apart," "designate," or "appoint" for a special function or office, but a special noun meaning "ordination" is not used in the Bible. However, the word "ordain" is used to translate the following words: *sim, sum* (Ps. 81:5, Hab. 1:12); *shapath* (Isa. 26:12); *poieo* (Mark 3:14); *krinein* (Acts 16:4); *horizein* (Acts 10:42); *cheirotonein* (Acts 14:23); *proorizein* (1 Cor. 2:7); *tassein* (Acts 13:48); *prographein* (Jude 4). "Ordain" is also used to translate Greek words meaning "to install" in office, or "consecrate," when the office is viewed as sacred, e. g. *kathistemi* (Heb. 5:1, Titus 1:5) and *diatasso* (1 Cor. 7:17).

Every solemn imposition of hands is not an act of ordination. The mothers brought their dear children to Christ "that He should put His hands on them, and pray" (Matt. 19:13). This was obviously an act of blessing, not ordaining. The early church practiced the imposition of hands upon the catechumens; upon the baptized in confirmation; and upon the penitents, in order to reconcile them with God; upon the sick, in order to advance their cure; upon any persons to give them a common benediction. These acts are not ordination in the sense we understand it. The imposition of hands upon the deaconesses was something still different from all these; the purpose was to consecrate them for a certain task in the church. Traditionally, an imposition of hands in this circumstance, along with a prayer of benediction for grace to discharge a task acceptably, has been intended as a consecration only. Thus it should be understood that the imposition of hands upon deaconesses is not an ordination providing full ecclesiastical authority.

Ellen White, commenting on Acts 13:2, provides us with reliable insight as to the ordination of ministers of the Gospel. "As they ministered to the Lord, and fasted, the Holy Ghost said, 'Separate Me Barnabas and Saul for the work whereunto I have called them.' Before being sent forth as missionaries to the heathen world, these apostles were solemnly dedicated to God by fasting and prayer and the laying on of hands. Thus they were authorized by the church, not only to teach the truth, but to perform the rite of baptism and to organize churches, being invested with full ecclesiastical authority" (White, *The Acts of the Apostles*, pp. 160, 161).

Note that the apostles were invested with full ecclesiastical authority. They were authorized by the church beyond teaching the truth, which is, as we understand teaching, a prerogative of every common faithful believer. They were authorized beyond that to baptize and organize churches. As we have seen, the apostle Paul does not recognize women teachers in the position of rabbis with ecclesiastical authority.

Ellen White further informs us: "He [God] instructed the church by revelation to set them apart publicly to the work of the ministry. Their ordination was a public recognition of their divine appointment … Both Paul and Barnabas had already received their commission from God Himself, and the ceremony of the laying on of hands added no new grace or virtual qualification. It was an acknowledged form of designation to an appointed office and a recognition of one's authority in that office. By it the seal of the church was set upon the work of God" (Ibid., pp. 161, 162).

Through the Holy Spirit, God calls people into His service. The Holy Spirit impresses people only in full harmony with the revealed principles of God's holy Word; the church recognizes their divine appointments and places her seal on God's work. It is, however, the solemn responsibility of the church to be very careful not to place her seal on that which is not sanctified as the work of God.

Women are not excluded from teaching and doing service in the church, nor from labor in the gospel ministry. Their services and labors are most welcome and much appreciated. However, there is no mandate that they should serve in these ways in positions of ordained leadership with full ecclesiastical authority.

The genuine gifts of the Spirit should be encouraged and should never be ignored or even suppressed. However, in this particular area, caution is very appropriate. The church cannot encourage or sanctify any gift that is, somehow, not in line with Biblical rule and teaching.

In the parable of the talents Jesus rewards the faithful worker with the words: "Well done, good and faithful servant: thou hast been faithful over a few things, I will make thee ruler over many things: enter thou into the joy of thy Lord" (Matt. 25:23). But to those with supposed or usurped gifts of the Spirit, although they have been very active and done great things, Jesus will say: "I never knew you: depart from me, ye that work iniquity" (Matt. 7:22, 23).

We can see that claiming a spiritual gift is a very serious matter that should be carefully studied in the light of God´s Word and seriously considered only if it matches the biblical standard. Any deviation from the biblical rule or teaching will surely result in loss and disaster. Those who are not justified to lead and rule the church according to the biblical standard, no matter how successful they might be, will eventually reap bitter disappointment.

The Bible teaches us many important lessons indicating that only unconditional obedience to God's commands and unreserved acceptance of His policies will bring about peace and happiness.

A dramatic incident that occurred when Israel was on the way to the Promised Land was the rebellion of Korah, who aspired to the dignity of the priesthood. He succeeded to secure on his side a vast number of fellow conspirators and sympathizers. In their blind presumption, they felt confident to pursue their course, and they provoked the Lord. But the whole rebellious company was met with a swift judgment, and they perished alive. But the seeds of rebellion were sown and the children of Israel gathered the next day against Moses and Aaron. God sent a plague and more than fourteen thousand of Israel died. Why was this impressive story recorded in the Bible? What is the lesson for later generations? It is a penetrating warning to God's people, "especially those who live upon the earth near the close of time" (White, *Counsels on Diet and Foods*, p. 428).

It is remarkable that quite a number of aspects of this story, as presented in the Bible and expressed in the Spirit of Prophecy, match several characteristics of the contemporary movement to ordain women leaders in the church. It certainly is to our benefit to contemplate the valuable lesson that is kept before us this way.

Chapter 14

A Striking Parallel

The following table compares aspects of the priesthood movement that was initiated by Korah with that of the contemporary ordination movement. The comparative aspects are based on Numbers 16 and statements in *Patriarchs and Prophets*, pages 395–405.

The Priesthood Movement	The Ordination Movement
Korah, though appointed to the service of the tabernacle, had become dissatisfied with his position and aspired to the dignity of the priesthood.	Though women are welcome to serve in the church, several are dissatisfied and aspire to the pastoral dignity of being ordained with full authority.
Aaron and Moses were not entitled to distinction above others in Israel; they were no more holy than the people, and it should have been enough for them to be on a level with their brethren, who were equally favored with God's special presence and protection. And so the priesthood should not be restricted to the house of Aaron.	No one in God's church is entitled to distinction above others. All are one in Christ, blessed and holy. All should be equally recognized by the church, including male and female persons. Women are, like men, called to leading positions of authority in the church. Ordination is not based on gender difference.

The Priesthood Movement	The Ordination Movement
Although they had no clear word of the Lord that justified their aspiration to the priesthood, they were sure they followed a right course.	Although there is no clear Biblical evidence that women should be ordained, many feel sure that they are right to promote such a move.
God had entrusted the priesthood to Aaron and his sons. They alone were chosen to administer this office.	God has revealed in His Word that only able men in the church are called as ordained leaders with full authority.
In order to achieve their goal, Korah and his company felt confident enough to make a radical change in the government.	Many feel confident enough to vote for a change in the constitution and bylaws to pave the way to ordain women.
They professed a great interest in the people. Prosperity would be certain if their scheme was followed. They really believed themselves to be actuated by a zeal for God.	Since the supporters of women's ordination believe that the Holy Spirit is leading them, they also believe that the church will prosper when ordination is made available to women.
Korah and his associates were moved more by feelings of dissatisfaction and the influence of circumstances than by the clear facts of truth.	Those in favor of women's ordination are moved more by feelings and the influence of popular opinion than by the convincing facts of biblical truth.
The princes felt confident that they were equally called with Aaron to the priesthood and they presented themselves presumptuously with their censers.	Gifted women are called equally with able men to be ordained as leaders in the church with full authority and they move boldly forward.

The Priesthood Movement	The Ordination Movement
Since there was no divine support for this movement, it was styled *rebellion,* which resulted in a dramatic disaster. Stubborn persistence sealed their doom.	If there is no biblical basis for ordaining women, a stubborn, persistent move to do so will be an act of rebellion that will eventually result in a great and terrible loss.

It is of crucial importance to consider these aspects carefully. Is it possible that the same evils that lay at the foundation of Korah's ruin still exist today? When we cherish pride and ambition, and try to reach positions God has not appointed for us, the soul will be alienated from God. It is the right of God not to call us all equally in His service. There are differences of role and position between men and women, apparent even before the fall.

Chapter 15

Differences

Before the fall there were some marked differences between Adam and Eve. Although Eve was cautioned for her own safety to beware of separating from her husband (White, *Patriarchs and Prophets*, p. 53), there was no need of imposed subjection of one to the other. Both were perfectly united under the direction of the Holy Spirit.

Through the fall a great change came. Ellen White writes: "Sin had brought discord, and now their union could be maintained and harmony preserved only by submission on the part of the one or the other … she [Eve] was now placed in subjection to her husband" (Ibid., p. 58). Before the fall there was perfect love and harmony without any discord. After the fall, discord came in and union could be maintained and harmony preserved *only* by submission; therefore, subjection was imposed. "Thy desire shall be to thy husband and he shall rule over thee" (Gen. 3:16). This divine law ruled humankind after the fall. Thus, there is a clear difference in the relationship of man and woman after the fall.

Referring to Creation in 1 Timothy 2:13, the apostle Paul makes it clear that the man was formed first: "For Adam was first formed, then Eve." Genesis emphasizes that the woman was created for the man. "And the Lord God said, It is not good that the man should be alone; I will make him a help meet for him" (Gen. 2:18). She was made from the rib of the man: "And the rib, which the Lord God had taken from man, made he a woman, and brought her unto the man" (Gen. 2:22). These passages reveal a pre-eminence of man in some sense although we should regard it as a pre-eminence of perfect love and harmony.

Does the Bible explicitly say that Adam and Eve were equal? Is the fact that both were appointed to have dominion over every living thing (Gen. 1:28), a clear indication of their mutual relationship of equality? In what sense were Adam and Eve equal? It is clear that Genesis 1:28 applies to both Adam and Eve: "And God blessed them, and God said unto them, Be fruitful, and multiply … and have dominion over the fish … and over every living thing that moveth upon the earth." If we want to have the Bible explain itself and have a clear understanding we should compare this text with the more detailed information given us in Genesis 2.

We read in Genesis 2:5: "And there was not a man to till the ground." Note that the Bible does not say: There was not a man and a woman to till the ground. Then the Bible says in verse 7: "And the Lord God formed man of the dust of the ground." Note that there is no reference yet to a woman. We then read in verse 8 that God planted a garden "and there he put the man whom He had formed." Note that the text does not say: And there He put the man and the woman. No, there was not yet a woman. Adam was introduced into the garden while he was alone, without a woman. In verse 15 the role of man is clearly stated: "And the Lord God took the man, and put him into the garden of Eden to dress it and to keep it." Ellen White says: "When God made man He made him ruler over the earth and all living creatures" (White, *Patriarchs and Prophets*, p. 59). In the following two verses the Lord God commanded the man that he might freely eat of every tree but not of the tree of the knowledge of good and evil "for in the day that thou eatest thereof thou shalt surely die" (verse 17). Thus man was placed into the garden and acquainted with God's purpose and will while he was still alone, without a woman.

Then the Lord God said in verse 18: "It is not good that the man should be alone; I will make him a help meet for him." God placed man in the garden to dress and keep it, gave him His instructions, and then provided man with a helpmate. However, before doing so, God brought every living creature unto Adam "to see what he would call them: and whatsoever Adam called every living creature, that was the name thereof … but for Adam there was not found a help meet for him" (verse 19). It was then that the Lord God took a rib from man and made a woman to be a helpmate for him.

Thus it is clear that Adam was created first, acquainted with God's purpose and commands, and given the privilege to provide all creatures with a name. Since she was formed after that, the woman had no share in these first acts. The woman was not created like man from the dust of the ground but from a rib of the man and she was almost a head shorter than man (White, *Conflict and Courage*, p. 11).

Eve was not formed as a man with a body like that of Adam, but as a woman with a different body. God created them "male and female" (Gen. 1:27). Their bodies were fitted for different roles. Thus, as we read in the next verse that God blessed them and said unto them, "Be fruitful, and multiply, and replenish the earth," we know and understand that each party plays a different role in this process as a *father* and a *mother*.

Thus the Bible establishes some essential differences instead of presenting this first couple as equal in form and role. Adam was on the scene before Eve and he was to till the ground; he was placed in the garden to cultivate it. He also named every living creature before the woman was given to him as a helpmate. The world of Adam was established first along with the purpose of living in that world; Eve, as Adam's helpmate, came into the world over which he had been given lordship. Although her position was special as his helpmate, and intimate as the mother of his children, he was in charge of the world as it was before the fall, including Eve. They were not equally autonomous.

Note that after the fall God said to Adam: "Cursed is the ground for thy sake … thorns also and thistles shall it bring forth to thee … In the sweat of thy face shalt thou eat bread" (Gen. 3:17–19). Thus after the fall, man's task, the tilling of the ground, was made more difficult because of the curse. Did God give the woman the same curse? No, God gave Eve a different but equal curse: "I will greatly multiply thy sorrow and thy conception; in sorrow thou shalt bring forth children" (Gen. 3:16).

The roles of the first man and woman are not identical. A close reading of Genesis, chapters 1–3, reveals that there are basic differences in the process of their creation which determine their relationship as a couple. If it is clear that Adam and Eve were not in all aspects *alike*, in what sense does Ellen White say that Eve is to stand by Adam's side "as an *equal*?" She says: "Eve was created from a rib taken from the side of Adam, signifying that she was not to control him as the head, nor to be trampled under his feet as an inferior, but to stand by his side as an equal, to be loved and protected by him" (White, *Patriarchs and Prophets*, p. 46). In other words, Adam was to respect and love Eve for who and what she was—as God loves and respects His created beings, whom He has created to be different from one another.

In this regard, note what Ellen White, for instance, says about John the

Baptist: "I saw that the humblest disciples who followed Jesus, witnessed His miracles, and heard the comforting words which fell from His lips, were greater than John the Baptist; that is, they were more exalted and honoured, and had more pleasure in their lives" (White, *Early Writings,* p. 155).

This statement seems to suggest a direct opposition to the words of Jesus recorded in Matthew 11:11: "Verily I say unto you, among them that are born of women there hath not risen a greater than John the Baptist." Ellen White says that some disciples were greater than John the Baptist, while Jesus says that there has been no one greater than John the Baptist. How can this be?

Was John the Baptist in all aspects great? No, he was not. Ellen White says that his life was sorrowful and lonely and he was not permitted to witness Christ's miracles and enjoy the power manifested by Him (White, *Early Writings,* p. 154). Thus, he was not great in this aspect but he was, however, great in his mission and nobility of character. Of this Ellen White writes: "John was great in the sight of the Lord, when, before the messengers from the Sanhedrin, before the people, and before his own disciples, he refrained from seeking honor for himself, but pointed all to Jesus as the Promised One. His unselfish joy in the ministry of Christ presents the highest type of nobility ever revealed in man" (White, *The Desire of Ages,* 219).

Likewise, Adam and Eve were not equal in all aspects, but there is equality between them in creation and in relation. Eve was not of a different species. She was made to be just as human as Adam was: "one who was fitted to be his companion, and who could be one with him in love and sympathy" (White, *Patriarchs and Prophets,* p. 46). She was "bone of his bone and flesh of his flesh" (Ibid.). "She was taken out of Man" (Gen. 2:23). Ellen White explains: "She was his second self, showing the close union and the affectionate attachment that should exist in this relation" (White, *Patriarchs and Prophets,* p. 46).

Through divine instruction, Israelite mothers also understood that boys and girls, men and women, were not equal in all aspects. At the birth of their children, they were immediately confronted with the difference between the two sexes as ordered by God's precept. Whatever the reason, God specified that when a male child was born, the period of purification was to last thirty-three days. However, when a female child was born, the period of purification was doubled and lasted sixty-six days (Lev. 12:1–5).

Thus, according to God's instruction, men and women are not placed on a completely equal platform.

Chapter 16

The Possibility of Creating a Schism

Some people argue that if we maintain that women cannot be ordained as pastors to use certain talents and gifts of organization and leadership, just because they are women, we may be anti-biblical and create a schism in the church. They say the Bible teaches that all should be one and so we should treat men and women alike. They say the issue is not a question of culture; therefore, based on this basic biblical principle, we should ordain women equally with men. But does the intended biblical unity of all include equal ordination?

I have reviewed some basic biblical principles, as presented by Paul, behind the opposite viewpoint: not to ordain women as pastors. Was Paul short-sighted? Are we more gifted than the apostle Paul? Was he not inspired by the Holy Spirit? Did he fear creating a possible schism when he instructed Timothy and Titus to appoint men and not women as elders and leaders in the church?

Should we argue against biblical instruction with our own thoughts? Should we try to make a different opinion or meaning acceptable, as if we could mold this clear teaching of the Bible as we please? Or should we humbly trust that God inspired and enlightened Paul's mind when he gave this instruction as being the unerring will and rule of God? Isn't it infinitely much better to take Paul's divinely inspired instructions seriously as God's holy words, which are "purified seven times" (Ps. 12:6), instead of coming up with our own human arguments and finite thoughts?

It is narrow-minded to assert that because a woman cannot be ordained as a pastor, she cannot use her talents in the church. It is shortsighted to conclude that there is no possibility for a woman to use her gifts of organization and leadership in the church if she does not use them to carry out the specific pastoral duties assigned to men in the Bible. There are many positions in the church that call for organizational and leadership skills, such as home missionary work; the work of Bible instructors; counseling work; social welfare work; the care of elderly members, the sick, and the needy; youth and children's activities; health care and medical missionary work; guiding the economic and financial policy of the church; public relations work; and the organization of various evangelistic activities. Women are not excluded from teaching and working in the gospel ministry. However, there is no mandate that they should serve in positions of ordained leadership, with full ecclesiastical authority.

The North American request for gender-inclusive ordination took center stage at the General Conference session in Utrecht on Wednesday afternoon, July 5, 1995. The request was made by Alfred McClure, president of the SDA church in North America. When the secret ballots were counted, 673 voted in favor, 1481 against. The proposal lost. The issue was clearly decided.

Note Alfred C. McClure's testimony: "Let it only be said that when this church came together in Utrecht around a potentially divisive matter, the Holy Spirit had His way, God made clear His will to the body, and the church came from the debate stronger, better able to accomplish its mission, and more closely united than ever before" (*Adventist Review*, August 3, 1995, p. 5).

Think about these words. The Lord has spoken. Did God speak for only a few years? Are we now, like Balaam, to tempt the Lord and have our own way?

Chapter 17

Home and Church

Other people argue that there is a marked difference in the home and in the church. If we insist on a different status of men and women than the one that exists in the home as the result of sin, and transfer it to the church organization, then we are working against the unity in the church for which Christ prayed and gave His life—that we may be saved and become one in Him.

If a woman in the family circle is expected to be submissive to her husband and regard him as head, could she then be a responsible and authoritative head and ruler in the church, as if different principles and rules apply there? Is there a conflict between home and church or is there harmony between the two?

There should be no conflict between the Christian home and the Christian church. Christ is the head of the church and man is the head of the family and he is to imitate Christ.

Ellen White explains: "The Lord has constituted the husband the head of the wife to be her protector; he is the house-band of the family, binding the members together, even as Christ is the head of the church and the Saviour of the mystical body. Let every husband who claims to love God, carefully study the requirements of God in his position. Christ's authority is exercised in wisdom, in all kindness and gentleness; so let the husband exercise his power and imitate the great Head of the church" (White, *The Faith I Live By*, p. 259).

Thus, when the husband follows Christ as his great example, Who "placed Himself at the head of the human family" (White, *Sons and Daughters of God*, p. 153); when he as father and head imitates the great Head of the church, there will be no conflict but harmony; the family will be in line with the church.

No wonder that Ellen White calls the family a home church: "Parents ... train for Him the little church in your home, that on the Sabbath all may be prepared to worship in the Lord's sanctuary" (White, *Testimonies for the Church*, vol. 6, p. 354). "Every family in the home life should be a church, a beautiful symbol of the church of God in heaven... I speak to fathers and mothers: You can be educators in your home churches; you can be spiritual missionary agencies" (White, *Child Guidance*, pp. 480, 481). "Those who govern their families in the right way will bring into the church an influence of order and reverence ... Model homes make a model church. Every family is a church, over which the parents preside ... When the father and mother as priest and teacher of the family take their position fully on the side of Christ, a good influence will be exerted in the home. And this sanctified influence will be felt in the church and will be recognized by every believer ... The home is a school where all may learn how they are to act in the church ... Let there be peace in the home, and there will be peace in the church" (Ibid., pp. 548, 549).

The Christian home on earth is a reflection of the family in heaven, and so is God's church. The home circle is like a little church, a model of the community church. There is no different foundation. Jesus Christ is the cornerstone of the family church as well as of the community church. There is a parallel between the home and the church instead of a fundamental difference. "The wife should see in her relation to her husband a reflection, or illustration, of her relation to Christ" (White, *The SDA Bible Commentary*, vol. 6, p. 1036).

> The headship of the husband consists in his ability and responsibility to care for his wife, in the same way that Christ cares for the church ... As Christ is the 'saviour of the body' the church, so the husband should be the protector and sustainer of his wife and family. No question of inferiority or of headship ever arises in a family where the husband shows the same solicitude for the welfare of his wife that Christ shows for His church ... the husband is to imitate Christ, giving up personal pleasures and comforts to obtain his wife's happiness, standing by her side in the hour of sickness. Christ gave Himself for the church because she was in desperate need. He did it to save her. Likewise the husband will give himself for the salvation of his wife,

ministering to her spiritual needs, and she to his, on a spirit of mutual love. (Ibid.)

Thus it is clear that there is agreement between the Christian home and God's church. No fundamental difference in the status of men and women at home or in the church would, by exchange, be a threat to the unity of Christ's church.

Chapter 18

Neither Male nor Female

Most people who think that the Bible is in harmony with the ordination of women for leading positions in the church refer to Galatians 3:27, 28 as their authority for this viewpoint: "For as many of you as have been baptized into Christ have put on Christ. There is neither Jew nor Greek, there is neither bond nor free, there is neither male nor female: for ye are all one in Christ Jesus."

What kind of unity is Paul speaking of in this passage? If we interpret the last phrase of this passage as teaching that there is no difference between men and women so that all ministries in the church are open to either sex, then the harmony of the Bible is clearly at stake. Elsewhere in his writings, the apostle Paul stressed some clear differences between men and women. For example, he instructed Timothy and Titus to appoint men, not women, as leaders in the church (1 Tim. 2:11-15; 3:1-7; Titus 1:5-9). Based on these passages that address the differences between men and women, why would Paul teach in Galatians 3:28 that there is no functional difference anymore between believers because the gospel of Jesus Christ took all distinction away? This is contrary to the teaching of the Bible and Paul's other writings.

If a Jew comes to Christ, is he still a Jew? Yes. If a Greek accepts Christ, is he still a Greek? Yes. This principle of distinction applies also to bond and free. And so it should be clear that there is still some distinction between the sexes. Thus, for believers in Christ the different social and ethnological positions and roles still remain. Although, through the influence of faith, these characteristics may change to some extent, they are not taken away. We observe that in Christ all are one, but all are not equal in all things. All are equivalent but not in function and position. Through faith in Christ all believers equally share, without any difference of nationality, social position, or gender, in the spiritual unity of the royal priesthood (1 Peter 2:9).

Unfortunately, the phrase "there is neither male nor female" is often used out of context to prove full equality of both sexes and to justify the ordination of women in the church to the gospel ministry. However, this passage speaks about being baptized into Christ and not about the ordination of men or women in the church. The passage confirms that those who accept Christ in their lives and those who call upon the name of the Lord (Rom. 10:13) will be saved. The passage assures us that salvation in Christ is not restricted to a certain class, nationality, or gender. All who call upon the Lord and all who are baptized in His name are all one in Him and will be equally saved. These texts speak about equal salvation in Christ for everyone.

These texts do not suggest that authority be attributed to men and women for occupying leading positions in the church. However, proponents of women's ordination argue that Christ's redeeming sacrifice saves men and women alike, thus restoring gender equality, which reflects on church ministry, and so women should be ordained equally with men. But is this a good and solid biblical point of view? Do we find clear evidence in the Bible that, as to serve the Lord in the various capacities, there is among believers no gender difference anymore? Does the fact that men and women are equally saved by faith in Christ really indicate that they can serve the Lord alike in any leading position in the church? Where do we find any evidence for that in the Bible? Can we maintain in the face of the Bible that being equally saved eliminates all role differences between men and women? As we have seen already, several Bible passages indicate a difference of position between men and women.

Likewise, the pen of inspiration informs us precisely about the procedure that the apostles carefully followed. "In the work of setting things in order in all the churches, and ordaining suitable men to act as officers, the apostles held to the high standards of leadership outlined in the Old Testament Scriptures" (White, *The Acts of the Apostles*, p. 95). Thus, it is clear that the Old Testament principles of male leadership still apply in New Testament times. And so we can be sure that no woman was appointed nor ordained as a leader in the church.

But didn't Christ pray for unity, that they all may be one? Does this not undo all differences? It should be clear that the unity for which Christ prayed is a unity in spirit and in truth, but not a unity of equal status and position in the church of men and women.

From the beginning Adam was appointed to be the head of the family. This was not the result of sin. "Under God, Adam was to stand at the head of the earthly family, to maintain the principles of the heavenly family" (White, *Reflecting Christ*, p. 51). "When God made man He made him ruler over the earth and all living creatures" (White, *Patriarchs and Prophets*, p. 59). Adam's status was ordained at the Creation, before the fall; these statements about his status do not mention the woman.

Thus, also before the fall, at their creation, man and woman were not in all points equal. The man was made head and ruler on the basis of perfect mutual love, but as a consequence of sin, we read that the desire of the woman shall be to her husband, who shall rule over her (Gen. 3:16). Thus, after the fall there was a definite subjection of the woman to the man.

Another argument put forward by some people is that the King James Bible indicates the ordination of many different inanimate things, such as *places* (1 Chron. 17:9); *peace* (Isa. 26:12); *musical instruments* (2 Chron. 29:27); *feasts* (1 Kings 12:33); and *one's status or condition* (1 Cor. 7:17). This being so, they conclude that when ordination is applied to a variety of lesser things or values, it should be no problem to ordain women, who are to be regarded as being on a much higher plane. However, it is obvious that the word "ordain," as used with regard to these inanimate "lesser" things, cannot have the same meaning when applied to living human beings set apart as responsible leaders in the church. There is no laying on of hands with the lesser things. There is no investing of full ecclesiastical authority as with men who are authorized by the church to perform all pastoral duties. Therefore, no equal comparison with an equal application and meaning is possible.

Chapter 19

A Biblical Concept of Inspiration

Proponents of women's ordination are often more inclined to interpret certain passages of the Bible according to principles rather than to what is literally said. They try to look beyond the plain, literal meaning of a passage to discover the involved principles operating behind the text.

However, as we consider this method, we must ask, Does this mean that people are more or less free to discover the principles they like most? And who determines what the right principles are and what precisely their meaning is so that a correct biblical interpretation and application in church ministry is assured?

To gain a better understanding, we should also consider how the proponents of women's ordination usually view the process of inspiration. Many do not only picture a special role for the Holy Spirit, but they also emphasize a particular role of influence on the text through the human author. They perceive biblical inspiration as a process by which God, through His Spirit, imparts a divine message to His servants who formulate it according to their own cultural, social, and historical settings.

Thus, they believe that the divinely inspired message contains a certain amount of human input, which could possibly make a literal interpretation, as being the pure word of God, undesirable, and in some cases it can be even misleading. A careful exegesis should be, therefore, applied that explores the historical, cultural, and social aspects of a passage.

Many feel that a literal application is not always intended to be applied in later ages but rather the broad principle behind a passage should be expressed and applied in the ministry of the church. Thus, a wider perspective is opened that supersedes the literal meaning. But how far could this go? And where does this end? And who decides all this? If we use this method of interpretation, are we not in danger of entering a wide field of uncertainty and unbiblical applications and possibilities that the human mind may device and prefer to apply? Who determines what should and should not be applied? And who is to set out exactly the amount and kind of human input in a Bible passage? These valid questions demand honest consideration.

It is true that the divine message is presented in human words, but could the Bible writers in some way influence the divine message more or less in their own way? Were they able to insert their own particular input in the inspired message? Note Ellen White's valuable comment: "God has been pleased to communicate His truth to the world by human agencies, and He Himself, by His Holy Spirit, qualified men and enabled them to do this work. He guided the mind in the selection of what to speak and what to write. The treasure was entrusted to earthen vessels, yet it is, nonetheless, from Heaven. The testimony is conveyed through the imperfect expression of human language; yet it is the testimony of God; and the obedient, believing child of God beholds in it the glory of a divine power, full of grace and truth" (White, *The Great Controversy 1888*, p. iv).

Ellen White states that God "Himself, by His Holy Spirit, *qualified* men and *enabled* them to" be God's agencies. She also wrote, "[God's] penman selected the most expressive language through which to convey the truths ..." (White, *Selected Messages,* book 1, p. 22). He *guided* the mind in the *selection* of what to speak and what to write. So we see that human agencies stand under direct influence of God, and thus, what they spoke and wrote was from Heaven. It is the testimony of God, full of grace and truth.

Is there any evidence in the Bible that inspired passages contain a certain amount of human input? Note the principle that Ellen White explained as to the prophet Balaam: "As he professed to be God's prophet, however, all he should say would be supposed to be uttered by divine authority. Hence he was not to be permitted to speak as he chose, but must deliver the message which God should give him" (White, *Patriarchs and Prophets*, p. 441).

It is clear that God's prophets are not permitted to add some of their own words to the divine message. Balaam was very eager to influence and formulate God's message according to king Balak's desires, and he tried desperately to do so. Three times he spoke, but he could not in any way succeed to alter or withhold God's message. "Balaam confessed that he came with the purpose of cursing Israel, but the words he uttered were directly contrary to the sentiments of his heart. He was constrained to pronounce blessings, while his soul was filled with curses" (Ibid., p. 447). "Again the prophet was entrusted with a divine message, which he was powerless to alter or withhold" (Ibid., p. 448).

Here we have a clear demonstration that even an unwilling prophet who cherished disagreeing thoughts and feelings could only speak the words that the Lord God gave him to proclaim. And so there is no doubt that "the Lord's controlling power was upon him" (Ibid., p. 443). Balaam stood, like other prophets of God, under the direct guidance and influence of God's Holy Spirit. Balaam was "moved by the Holy Ghost" (2 Peter 1:21), and the message he brought was the undefiled testimony of God, full of grace and truth.

Although Balaam, in his passion for honor and riches, did his very utmost to comply with king Balak's wishes, he was, on the other hand, well aware that he could not in any way influence nor resist the divine message that God would give him to speak. He answered Balak's servants: "If Balak would give me his house full of silver and gold, I cannot go beyond the word of the Lord my God, to do less or more" (Num. 22:18). And to Balak he said: "Lo, I am come unto thee: have I now any power at all to say any thing? the word that God putteth in my mouth, that shall I speak" (Num. 22:38).

Balaam knew the truth. He knew he had no power at all to say what king Balak wanted him to say. He had to proclaim God's message. He could not withhold something nor add anything, and so we can be sure that the divine message that God gave to His servants to speak or to write down is pure and undefiled, without human input. This is what makes the Bible the most outstanding book in the world. This is what makes it possible to testify, as Ellen White did, "Perfect excellence is found only in the word of the living God" (White, *Counsels to Writers and Editors*, p. 121). This testimony certainly would not be true if God's writers could have, in any way, added their own words.

Another example is the prophet Jeremiah who had to proclaim a message of reproof and who was, because of this, daily derided and mocked. How gladly would he have toned down God's divine message to a more agreeable level. Was he able to influence God's divine message in his own way? Apparently not. "From the messages given him he must diminish not a word..." (White, *Prophets and Kings*, p. 412.) And so, he proclaimed God's message plain and unvarnished, but at a certain moment he could not stand it any longer, and he declared, "I will not make mention of him, nor speak any more in his name" (Jer. 20:9). Could Jeremiah keep this decision?

Ellen White comments: "But what did this prophet of the Lord do after his decision? Try as much as he would, he could not hold his peace. As soon as he came into the assemblies of the people, he found that the Spirit of the Lord was stronger than he was. The record is: 'His word was in mine heart as a burning fire shut up in my bones, and I was weary with forbearing, and I could not stay'" (White, *The SDA Bible Commentary*, vol. 4, p. 1156).

Here again we have clear evidence that in the process of inspiration the Holy Spirit is stronger than the human spirit and will. God's human servants can do their utmost to withhold the divine message, but they cannot prevail. Did God's human servants in any way add their own input to the divine message? No, God's word was in Jeremiah's heart as a burning fire, and so, the prophet could not hold his peace, and he proclaimed God's plain and unadulterated message. This proves that we have a sure and solid divine foundation for our faith to build upon.

Thus, the biblical process of inspiration provides no evidence of human input in a literal passage that would influence its interpretation in such a way that a clear, plausible, literal application should be viewed as undesirable, which would make it particularly advisable to look for a broad principle-based explanation and application.

Note Ellen White's recommendable attitude toward the Bible. She testified: "I take the Bible just as it is, as the Inspired Word. I believe its utterances in an entire Bible" (White, *Selected Messages,* book 1, p. 17). She advised: "Brethren, cling to your Bible, as it reads ..." (Ibid., p. 18). And she warned: "Human reasoning and the imaginings of the human heart are undermining the inspiration of the Word of God, and that which should be received as granted, is surrounded with a cloud of mysticism. Nothing stands out in clear and distinct lines, upon rock bottom. This is one of the marked signs of the last days" (Ibid., p. 15).

Let us take the Bible as it reads, and let us be careful not to mystify its plain meaning according to our own ideas, wishes, and preferences. Let the truths of the Bible stand out clearly, unmixed with modern cultural views or doubtful interpretations, theories, suggestions and suppositions.

Chapter 20

Reputable Women in the Bible

In the New Testament, we find several examples of women who were actively involved in church matters. Some were eyewitnesses of Christ's death and burial. Women were the first to note the empty tomb and resurrection of Christ. Women were also the first to proclaim the message of the risen Lord to the disciples. Women played a prominent part in several important events in the life of Christ and in the early church. They exerted a good influence on the growth of the church.

However, does this mean that women are qualified to be ordained in the gospel ministry? If so, why then were they not actually appointed, equally with men, in the pastoral ministries of the early church? Was it because of the social customs, circumstances, and cultural influences of the day? We must dismiss this thought because the Bible is a guide for all people, irrespective of culture, customs, and popular opinion.

Prophetic gift. Some women, in the early church, shared the prophetic gift. Joel prophesied that "it shall come to pass afterward, that I will pour out my spirit upon all flesh; and your sons and your daughters shall prophesy, your old men shall dream dreams, your young men shall see visions: And also upon the servants and upon the handmaids in those days will I pour out my spirit" (Joel 2:28, 29). Here we see that the outpouring of God's Spirit is not restricted to men only. All flesh would equally share in the promised outpouring.

On the day of Pentecost a clear fulfillment of Joel's prophecy was witnessed (Acts 2:16–18)—women also received the Spirit of God. Is this not a good argument that they could be ordained to the pastoral ministry of the gospel? We should notice, however, that the outpouring of God's Spirit on men and women is not dependent upon the act of ordination nor is ordination a prerequisite to receive the Holy Spirit. We must realize that ordination is not a necessary act to serve God.

There were undoubtedly many dedicated women in the early church who did a wonderful work and conscientiously served their Lord. Was the apostle Paul, who was the most prominent leader in the early church, not aware of this fact? Of course he was informed of this. He traveled around establishing and visiting many churches, and he stayed for months and sometimes even years in some churches to build them up and to provide them with divine counsel and instruction, and yet he did not instruct any church to appoint women leaders. Why not? Was the time not yet ripe for such a move? Was Paul perhaps held back in his teaching and instruction by popular, cultural, and social insights, as many believe and defend? If the apostles were led by public opinion in their dealings with the various churches, then, as we have stated earlier, the Bible would be a culturally bound product of the time, which could not serve as a sufficient and adequate guide for all people throughout all ages.

Divine power alone. We are assured, however, that Paul "claimed no wisdom of his own, but acknowledged that divine power alone had enabled him to present the truth in a manner pleasing to God. United with Christ, the greatest of all teachers, Paul had been enabled to communicate lessons of divine wisdom, which met the necessities of all classes, and which were to apply at all times, in all places, and under all conditions" (White, *The Acts of the Apostles*, p. 303).

Thus, there is no need, whatsoever, to doubt the accuracy of the Scriptures as being the sole Word of God. Not the influence of public opinion, but divine power *alone* enabled Paul to present the truth. And so, Paul could, concerning his instructions to the church, confidently testify "that the things that I write unto you are the commandments of the Lord" (1 Cor. 14:37).

Unnecessary burdens. We are also assured that Paul "had been taught by God regarding the binding of unnecessary burdens … and took a firm and unyielding position which brought to the churches freedom from Jewish rites and ceremonies" (White, *The Acts of the Apostles*, p. 200).

Now if it were true that women were indeed unjustly treated and bound by unnecessary burdens, then undoubtedly, God would have taught Paul about this matter also, for He is not careless nor partial, and we would not expect Paul to have been half-hearted in this matter. The apostles were "endued with power from on high" (Luke 24:49). "The Holy Spirit was to be given them in its fullness, sealing them for their work" (Ibid., p. 30). They were particularly guided and enabled by the Holy Spirit to be workers together with God as the foundation of the New Testament church was laid, built up and set forth as a divine model for later ages. We just cannot accept the idea that the foundation was defectively laid somehow, leaving women in a position of unjust treatment. Just as with the unnecessary Jewish burdens, Paul would have certainly addressed this issue as well and also taken a firm and unyielding stand on the position of women in serving the church. Since it touches a fundamental principle of humanity, he would definitely have brought freedom to women from their undue limitations and wrong insights regarding their functional inequality with men. Unquestionably he would have opened to them the ministerial offices in the church. However that did not happen in any way, so we can confidently accept that there is no ground to believe that the teaching of the Bible justifies the appointment and ordination of women as leaders in the church.

Paul taught and acted by principle. There is no doubt that Paul was guided and instructed by the Holy Spirit. He acted, directed, and counseled only by principle. He fully believed and respected God's sentence as pronounced upon Eve, and consequently he taught women to be submissive to their husbands. As to the position of women in the church, he referred to this pronounced law, the Creation and the fall. Paul also pointed out other differences in his letters, elaborating on the principle that God set forth when He disciplined Adam and Eve. Man was created first and the woman second; she was made from man and was to be his helper. Man was created in the image of God in a direct way while the woman was created in God's image via her husband. The woman was first to sin and she deceived her husband to sin also. God told the woman that she would be subordinate to her husband while the man would be the head of his family and have authority over his wife and household.

Order of Creation. It should not be neglected that Paul based the subordination of women not only on God's pronounced sentence but also on the Creation. Paul plainly stated: "... the head of the woman is the man...." and he explained: "For a man indeed ought not to cover his head, forasmuch as he is the image and glory of God: but the woman is the glory of the man. For the man is not of the woman; but the woman of the man. Neither was the man created for the woman; but the woman for the man" (1 Cor. 11:3, 7-9). These words directly refer to the order of creation and imply man's pre-eminence and woman's submission. It does not make sense to ignore these plain words or interpreted them otherwise. Nor does it make sense to argue that there was before the fall complete equality between Adam and Eve, for this is not in harmony with the Bible and it does not agree with Paul's teaching.

The aspects of the sentence, the creation and the fall, were clearly underlined by Paul and therefore they are not taken away by the gospel of Christ. And so in this context there is no change in the position of women that would justify women's ordination to the pastoral ministry.

Ministers of the gospel. No wonder the apostles were very careful to act according to the principles of the Bible in choosing only men as ministers of the gospel. Ellen White has this to say about the subject: "He [Paul] and Barnabas retraced their steps and visited the churches they had raised up, choosing from them men whom they could train to unite in proclaiming the gospel….The apostle made it a part of his work to educate young men for the office of the ministry" (Ibid., pp. 367, 368).

"Ministry comprehends far more than preaching the word. It means training young men as Elijah trained Elisha, taking them from their ordinary duties, and giving them responsibilities to bear in God's work…" (White, *Prophets and Kings*, p. 222). Thus, in training men for the ministry, the apostles followed also Elijah's example. God expects the church to do the same as Elijah, Christ and the apostles by training young men for the office of the ministry. "God calls for you, young men. He calls for whole armies of young men who are large-hearted and large-minded, and who have a deep love for Christ and the truth" (White, *Gospel Workers*, p. 63).

The apostles worked and acted in harmony with Christ's teachings, the great Head of the church: "The great Head of the church superintends His work through the instrumentality of men ordained by God to act as His representatives" (White, *The Acts of the Apostles*, p. 360). "God is calling for men … to become missionaries for Him…. In the past there have been men who, stirred by the love of Christ and the needs of the lost, have left the comforts of home and the society of friends, even that of wife and children … to proclaim the message of mercy" (Ibid., p. 370).

Full-time ministry. When Ellen White speaks about the gospel ministry in more general terms, she usually addresses, without regard to gender, all believers, including part time workers and lay members. However, in the specific context of full time gospel ministry, she speaks of men only, using masculine nouns. Could we regard this as a matter of chance?

As to Christ's specific command she says: "How broad and extended the command is, 'Go ye therefore, and teach all nations, baptizing them in the name of the Father, and of the Son, and of the Holy Ghost … What honor is here conferred upon man, and yet how large a number hug the shore! How few will launch out into the deep, and let down their nets for a draught! Now, if this is done, if men are laborers together with God, if men are called to act in city missions, and to meet all classes of minds, there should be special preparations for this kind of work" (White, *Fundamentals of Christian Education*, pp. 121, 122). Note also this statement: "In commissioning His disciples to go 'into all the world, and preach the gospel to every creature,' Christ assigned to men the work of spreading the gospel" (White, *Testimonies for the Church*, vol. 4, p. 472).

Ellen White wrote several statements where she clearly identified full-time gospel ministry with men. Note also how she does not speak of men and women but only of men in a passage that implies ordination:

> The apostle says, "Lay hands suddenly on no man." [1 Timothy 5:22.] In the days of the apostles, the ministers of God did not dare to rely upon their own judgment in selecting or accepting men to take the solemn and sacred position of mouthpiece for God. They chose the men whom their judgment accepted, and then placed them before the Lord to see if He would accept them to go forth as His representatives. No less than this should be done now.
>
> In many places we meet men who have been hurried into responsible positions as elders of the church, when they are not qualified for such a position…. Hands have been laid too suddenly upon these men.
>
> Ministers of God should be men of good repute … We stand in great need of competent men, who will bring honor instead of disgrace upon the cause which they represent.

All these things should be carefully and prayerfully considered before men are sent into the field of labor. (White, *Gospel Workers*, pp. 438, 439)

Thus we see again that Ellen White clearly associates ordination to the gospel ministry with men.

Delegated power and authority. Jesus, our great example and teacher, chose only men as His disciples, and He Himself endowed them with authority and ordained them to the gospel ministry: "When Jesus had ended His instruction to the disciples, He gathered the little band close about Him, and kneeling in the midst of them, and laying His hands upon their heads, He offered a prayer dedicating them to His sacred work. Thus the Lord's disciples were ordained to the gospel ministry" (White, *The Desire of Ages*, p. 296). This certainly was a very important act, but note that the ordained disciples were to delegate the divine power and authority to other consecrated men who were called to the gospel ministry. Christ promised His disciples: "Lo, I am with you always, even unto the end of the world" (Matt. 28:20). Ellen White, quoting this promise, explained: "He has ordained that there should be a succession of men who derive authority from the first teachers of the faith for the continual preaching of Christ and Him crucified. The Great Teacher has delegated power to His servants, who 'have this treasure in earthen vessels'" (White, *Testimonies for the Church*, vol., 4, p. 529).

Thus there should be "a succession of men" who derive their authority from the first teachers to preach the gospel of Christ and Him crucified. Believing that Ellen White was inspired as God's servant, it is noteworthy and meaningful that she associated the call to full-time gospel ministry with men and not with women. Was she wrong, and did she unjustly belittle the position and rights of women? Note, however, that she took a firm and decided stand as to the position of wives of ministers who were actively involved in their husband's work, and she pleaded their case that their consecrated labors should be recognized and paid for. She was certainly sympathetic to the needs and rights of women, but she never pleaded that women, equally with men, should be appointed and ordained as leaders of the church. This significant fact should not be overlooked but receive due consideration.

Ministry of men and women. All this, however, does not exclude women to work in the gospel ministry, for Ellen White also stated: "Everyone has his appointed work in the great field; and yet none should receive the idea that God is dependent upon man" (Ibid., p. 472). Thus, it should be clear that although women are not called and set apart by ordination for pastoral or full-time gospel ministry, there is an appointed work for them to do in this field. Ellen White explained: "The Saviour's commission to the disciples includes all believers to the end of time. All to whom the heavenly inspiration has come are put in trust with the gospel. All who receive the life of Christ are ordained to work for the salvation of their fellow men" (White, *Counsels to Parents, Teachers, and Students,* p. 466). Ellen White made this statement in the context of Christ's commission to the seventy who were also commissioned to heal the sick (Luke 10:9). The medical ministry is an important part of the gospel in which men and women should be active workers for God.

In another statement Ellen White said:

> It is a fatal mistake to suppose that the work of soul-saving depends alone upon the ministry. The humble, consecrated believer upon whom the Master of the vineyard places a burden for souls is to be given encouragement by the men upon whom the Lord has laid larger responsibilities. Those who stand as leaders in the church of God are to realize that the Saviour's commission is given to all who believe in His name. God will send forth into His vineyard many who have not been dedicated to the ministry by the laying on of hands....
>
> Let them understand that there is a large work to be done outside the pulpit by thousands of consecrated lay members.... When the members of the church of God do their appointed work in the needy fields at home and abroad, in fulfillment of the gospel commission, the whole world will soon be warned and the Lord Jesus will return to this earth with power and great glory. (White, *The Acts of the Apostles,* pp. 110, 111)

Thus, besides the full-time ordained male ministers upon whom God has laid larger responsibilities, there should be many dedicated men and women actively working as lay members in God's vineyard. The mission to proclaim the saving message of the kingdom of God rests upon all believers, and they should use their talents and every opportunity to witness to the love of God, making known God's saving grace and glorifying His name.

Priscilla. In the New Testament we have some great examples of dedicated women who were active gospel workers; however, their example has often unduly been used as an argument for the ordination of women. Many argue that Priscilla, for instance, together with her husband, Aquila, worked in the gospel ministry, and so provision should be made for women to be appointed as ministers in the church. It should be noted, however, that this couple was not chosen and set apart for a full-time ministry like the apostles were.

Priscilla and Aquila were tentmakers in Corinth, and Paul, being of the same craft, lived and worked with them for some time while he instructed them more perfectly in the truths of God's kingdom. Thus, this couple was well educated and established in the gospel of Christ, and while they carried on their business, they witnessed faithfully of the truths they had learned. Ellen White explains: "Aquila and Priscilla were not called to give their whole time to the ministry of the gospel, yet these humble laborers were used by God to show Apollos the way of truth more perfectly. The Lord employs various instrumentalities for the accomplishment of His purpose, and while some with special talents are chosen to devote all their energies to the work of teaching and preaching the gospel, many others, upon whom human hands have never been laid in ordination, are called to act an important part in soulsaving" (Ibid., p. 355).

Thus, we see that women, although they are not called to be ordained to the ministry, can nevertheless do a great and very important work for God.

Dorcas. Another example is Dorcas, a beloved woman who lived in Joppa. She was a faithful follower of Christ who performed many good deeds and acts of kindness. She lovingly attended to the physical needs of the poor. Ellen White wrote, "She knew who needed comfortable clothing and who needed sympathy, and she freely ministered to the poor and the sorrowful. Her skillful fingers were more active than her tongue" (Ibid., p. 131).

Dorcas is a good example of practical Christianity. Her service in the church covered a very important part of the gospel message, which marked the difference between a vain and a genuine religion. Dorcas exercised a living faith (James 2:17, 20) and practiced a pure and undefiled religion before God and the Father in visiting the poor and providing for their needs (James 1:27).

Although Dorcas' valuable ministry was of great influence to the advancement of the gospel message, there is no evidence that she was ordained or appointed to a responsible position in the church.

Lydia. We also have the example of Lydia, a seller of purple, from the city of Thyatira. She possessed the gift of hospitality, and she made a positive impact for the cause of God. She heard the apostles preach at Philippi, and she gladly accepted the truths of the gospel. She and her household were converted and baptized, and she kindly invited the apostles to make her house their home. Her hospitality was like a haven of shelter for the new converts, and when Paul and Silas were released from prison in Philippi, they rejoiced and went straight to Lydia's house where they met the group of new believers. Lydia was without a doubt a dedicated woman to God's cause, but we do not have any information that she became a leader of the Philippian church and was ordained as such.

Deborah. Although advocates of women ordination may admit that there is no clear evidence in the New Testament that women were ordained as leaders in the church, yet many of them are usually quick to refer to the Old Testament and point out that Deborah, a prophetess, "judged Israel… and the children of Israel came up to her for judgment" (Judges 4:4, 5). Here we have a clear example of a woman who was a leader in Israel and they argue that God is not changed and therefore it is no problem to have women leaders in our days as well. Is this not a strong argument to freely ordinate women to responsible, leading positions in the church?

When we consider this argument there are a few things that should draw our attention. The period of the Judges was now and then rather unruly. At a certain moment we read: "Every man did that which was right in his own eyes" (Judges 17:6). It could well be that such was the situation also in the days of the prophetess Deborah.

No magistrates. Ellen White informs us: "She was known as a prophetess, and in the absence of the usual magistrates, the people had sought to her for counsel and justice" (*The Signs of the Times*, June 16, 1881). This statement explains a lot. Why did the people come to Deborah? Was it because she was an appointed magistrate, judge or leader in Israel? The reason given us why people came to her is simply because there were no magistrates to go to! They were absent. Would this not tend to create an unruly situation? Is it then any wonder that the people came to Deborah? Where else should they go? Deborah was a prophetess, "a woman illustrious for her piety" (Ibid). And so, in the absence of magistrates, it is understandable that the people sought to her for counsel and justice expecting that she would, as a true prophetess, correct abuses and redress grievances.

There is no indication that any civil authority was conferred upon Deborah nor do we have any evidence that she was appointed as a magistrate or as a leader in Israel. But did God not chose her to deliver Israel from the yoke of the oppressor? In what sense was she chosen? Did God chose her to be the leader of Israel's army?

Barak. God told Deborah to instruct Barak to make war with king Jabin. Barak would win the battle and Sisera, the captain of Jabin's army, would be delivered into his hand. Not Deborah but Barak was Israel's leader and he is the one mentioned in Hebrews 11:32. Barak feared God and God could use him in spite of the fact that at the outset of his calling to deliver Israel, he lacked faith and was not very courageous.

Note Ellen White's comment: "Although he had been designated by the Lord Himself as the one chosen to deliver Israel, and had received the assurance that God would go with him and subdue their enemies, yet he was timid and distrustful…. He refused to engage in such a doubtful undertaking unless Deborah would accompany him…. Deborah consented, but assured him that because of his lack of faith, the victory gained should not bring honor to him; for Sisera would be betrayed into the hands of a woman" (Ibid., Judges 4: 6-9). Thus, there is no doubt that Barak was the appointed leader of Israel's army and it was because of his distrustful unbelief and lack of courage that Deborah took an encouraging part in the war against the enemy.

When we consider the situation and the circumstances under which Deborah as God's prophetess judged Israel, it is difficult to view her as a good and sound example in favor of appointing women to leading positions in the church. Christ and the apostles were certainly aware of Deborah's prophetic role in Israel, but none of them ever referred to her to plead a better position of women or to secure for them a leading role.

Conclusion. The ordination of women should not be based on contemporary ideas or socio-cultural norms, but it should be viewed in the light of the teaching of the whole Bible. That only men were ordained to full-time gospel ministry is in harmony with the revealed will of God and Christ's course of action, whose example and instructions the apostles carefully followed.

Chapter 21

Junia, a Woman Apostle?

Some people refer to Romans 16:7 where, they assert, a woman apostle is indicated: "Salute Andronicus and Junia, my kinsmen, and my fellow prisoners, who are of note among the apostles, who also were in Christ before me." This Bible text, undoubtedly, would be a strong support in favor of ordination of women in leadership if it were true and certain that:

1. Junia(s) was indeed a woman.
2. That she was indeed an apostle.
3. That the word *apostolos* is used in the sense of including leadership. A wider use of the word *apostolos* usually does not include leadership. "In the NT, (apostolos) can also mean delegate, envoy, messenger ... missionary" (Arndt, *A Greek-English Lexicon of the New Testament*, p. 99).

Henry Alford's *The Greek Testament* notes that Junias may be feminine from Junia or masculine from Junianus. Furthermore, as to the second point, two renderings are possible: "of note among the apostles, so that they themselves are counted among the Apostles ... or, noted among the apostles, i.e. well known and spoken of by the Apostles" (Alford, *The Greek Testament* vol. II, pp. 466, 467).

The Expositor's Greek Testament has similar notes, but with the more specific indication that the name Junias is probably masculine. It should also be noted that "it might mean, well-known to the apostolic circle, or distinguished as apostles" (Nicoll, vol. II, p. 719). The meaning of *apostolos* "implies, of course, a wide sense of the word Apostle" (Ibid.). However, "Scholars like Weiss and Gifford hold that what is meant here is that Andronicus and Junias were honourably known to the Twelve" (Ibid.).

The Translator's New Testament says, "The Greek is not clear. Either Paul thought of Andronicus and Junias as 'apostles' themselves, or he is stating that the apostles 'thought well of them'" (Bradnock, p. 474). Thus we do not have a solid, straightforward interpretation, when we assert that Junia(s) was a leading feminine apostle in the early church.

This controversial interpretation has strong adherents on both sides, but it should be noted that there is a modern trend that favors a feminine apostle. Most older commentators, however, take the name to be masculine. Several Bible translations also favor the masculine version:

- *The Twentieth Century New Testament:* "Andronicus and Junias, my countrymen and once my fellow prisoners, who are men of note among the Apostles …"
- *The Revised Standard Version*: "They are men of note among the apostles."
- *Goodspeed*: "They are noted men among the missionaries."
- *Philipps:* "They are outstanding men among the messengers."
- The Dutch translation (Nieuwe Vertaling) also indicates that Andronicus and Junias were both men.

Albert Barnes in his *Notes on the New Testament*, Romans 16:7, explains:

> Among the apostles - This does not mean that they *were* apostles, as has been sometimes supposed. For, (1.) There is no account of their having been appointed as such. (2.) The expression is not one which would have been used if they had been. It would have been 'who were distinguished apostles;' comp. Rom. i. 1; 1 Cor. i. 1; 2 Cor. i, 1; Phil. i. 1. It by no means implies that they were apostles. All that the expression fairly implies is, that they were known to the other apostles; that they were regarded by them as worthy of their affection and confidence; that they had been known by them, as Paul immediately adds, before he was himself

converted. (p. 328)

The Pulpit Commentary explains: "These men were in the confidence and esteem of the apostles. Some have inferred from the language used that Andronicus and Junias were numbered among the apostles, in the wider sense of that term. But it is more probable that they are mentioned as held in high respect and honour among the apostles generally" (Spence, vol. 18, p. 461).

Other sources that clearly favor the masculine identity of Andronicus and Junias could be cited. These sources also suggest that the men were not apostles but that they were highly esteemed by the apostolic circle.

Commenting on Romans 16:7, Chrysostom, however, wrote the following about Junia: "Oh! how great is the devotion of this woman, that she should be even counted worthy of the appellation of apostle" (Schaff, *A Select Library of the Nicene and Post-Nicene Fathers of the Christian Church*, p. 555). It should be noted that Chrysostom was not supported by everyone for this interpretation.

It is not in harmony with the historical facts of the early church that women would be appointed to ecclesiastical offices reserved for men. However, their gifts in serving the church were acknowledged and appreciated: "In general, woman's service was naturally along womanly lines, hospitality, care of the poor, the sick, prisoners and orphans, the oversight and instruction of women and children, and the last offices to the dead ... In the apostolic period women instructed new converts (Acts xviii. 26), they also spoke in meetings. The daughters of Philip (Acts xxi. 8-9) were not the only prophetesses. Christianity was in the outset charismatic, and women shared in these gifts" (Jackson, *The New Schaff-Herzog Encyclopedia of Religious Knowledge*, p. 414).

"Tertullian (De baptismo, xvii.) allowed laymen to baptize, but expressly forbade women both to baptize and to teach. The Apostolic Constitutions (iii. 9; also Origen, Homily on Isaiah vi.) state expressly that deaconesses were not to serve at the altar, and forbid them to teach and baptize or in any wise perform the functions of the priest" (Ibid., vol. 3, p. 375).

Joseph Bingham points out that the ministries of women in the Church were of great value but also that women were not allowed to occupy ministerial offices that had been assigned to men, such as the authority to baptize in particular:

The next question is concerning the baptism of women, whether they had any authority, or were ever allowed in any case to baptise in the Church? as to ordinary cases, it is agreed on all hands, that they were absolutely forbidden to meddle with any ecclesiastical office, and baptism in particular ... Tertullian ... forbids it absolutely to be done by women; and he goes upon this principle, that men were called to the sacerdotal office, but not women ... He calls it petulancy in women to usurp the power of baptizing ... Neither might they offer the oblation, nor assume to themselves any office belonging to men, much less those that appertained to the priests only... Nor does St. Jerom, nor St. Austin, nor Gelasius, nor Isidore, grant any authority to women to baptize, as they do to men ... Tertullian, Cyprian, and Firmilian ... are so peremptory in prohibiting women universally to meddle with the ministerial offices, and this always without exception of any cases whatsoever. (Bingham, *Origines Ecclesiasticae, or the Antiquities of the Christian Church and Other Works*, vol. 3, pp. 48–51)

No wonder that officially in the fourth Council of Carthage (Con. Carth. IV. Can. 100), women are absolutely forbidden to baptize, without any exception. Nevertheless, it is true that a number of the early Church Fathers understood Junias to be a woman, or the wife of Andronicus, thus a couple, like Priscilla and Aquila. This view is still held and advocated by many, and often the impression is given that the early church and all Church Fathers unanimously considered Junia(s) a woman. This, however, is not a truly objective view. Not all Church Fathers agreed on this point. Many of them don't even mention the issue at all, so we don't have their opinion. However, Origen as well as Epiphanius, for instance, clearly understood Junias to be a man.

Origen, being one of the earliest Church Fathers (circa AD 185–252), was one of the most proficient scholars of the ancient world; therefore, his viewpoint should be regarded as valuable. In his Latin commentary on Romans, he writes the name Junias in a masculine form (Migne, *Patrologia Graeca*, vol. 14, col. 1289). The name Junias, presented by Origen as a Latin masculine singular nominative, indicates that he believed Junias to be a man.

Epiphanius (315–403), early church historian and bishop of Salamis, wrote very specifically in his Index discipulorum: "Junias, whom Paul also mentions, became bishop of Apameia of Syria" (Burer, "Was Junia Really an Apostle? A Reexamination of Romans 16:7," *Journal of Biblical Manhood and Womanhood*). It is without doubt that Epiphanius identified Junias as a man, since the nominative form of the name as well as the relative pronoun is masculine.

However, it is argued that Epiphanius identified Prisca incorrectly as being a man and because of this mistake, his information about Junias should be dismissed as being unreliable. But when a mistake is detected, is it fair to regard everything else as being mistaken as well? This attitude does not seem to be well balanced. Epiphanius does not have a general reputation for being untrustworthy, so there is no particular reason to believe that he made many mistakes, and that he must also have incorrectly identified Junias as male. Other sources also identify Junias as a male bishop in Syria. The name "more probably represents a nominative Ioynias, an abbreviated form of Junianus … It has been conjectured from the name that he may have been originally a slave; the word 'kinsman' seems to suggest that he was of Jewish birth… In the list of the seventy by Pseudo-Dorotheus (A) Junias figures as bishop of Apamea in Syria" (Cheyne, *Encyclopaedia Biblica*, column 2646). According to the ancient coptic *Arabo Jacobite Synaxarium*, a volume with biographical information of saints, both Andronicus and Junias were male apostles. Andronicus "took with him Junias" and Junias "joined the apostle Andronicus … these two saints are mentioned by the apostle Paul" and Romans 16:7 is quoted. (Graffin, *Patrologia Orientalis*, Tomus Decimus Sextus, Chapter II, pp. 405–407).

Another fact to consider in relation to Junias is that most Church Fathers wrote in Latin, several centuries after Paul wrote his letter in Greek to the Romans. This difference in time and of language could possibly have resulted in some misunderstanding as to the correct gender of Junias.

Furthermore, there is some evidence that often information is borrowed from earlier sources. If this is the case with this issue, which is clearly suspected, then there is no possible ground to regard the later Church Fathers as being separate witnesses, since they only reflected the view of an earlier author. And it is accepted as being quite certain that they borrowed their information about Junias from Chrysostom, who understood Junias to be a woman (Schulz,

"Romans 16:7, Junia or Junias?" *The Expository Times: International Journal of Biblical Studies, Theology and Ministry,* p. 110).

Origen, Epiphanius and Chrysostom, should receive due attention since their testimony concerning Junias is more original than that of the other Church Fathers. To our knowledge, Origen should be regarded as the earliest, most valuable source, while the other two were the first ones who wrote in Greek about Junias.

Chrysostom, however, wrote rather late, some 350 years after Paul wrote his letter to the Romans, when the Greek language in the West was not popular anymore. As mentioned earlier, because of this, Chrysostom could possibly have mistaken the name to be feminine and if that is indeed the case, then he influenced later writers accordingly.

In any case, some valid questions remain. Was Chrysostom well informed about Junias? Did he consult all possible sources that were available? Was he aware of what Origen and Epiphanius had written? Chrysostom does not provide us with any more information except that he understood Junias to be Junia, a female apostle. He does not give us any explanation for this point of view. It is believed, however, that Chrysostom viewed Junia as an "apostle" in the wider sense and not as holding a position of influence and leadership in the church.

According to some, another important fact is that the older Greek minuscule manuscripts, which began having accents in the ninth century, denote that the name Junia(s) or 'Iounian' is masculine. "If jIounian should have the circumflex over the ultima (jIounia'n) then it is a man's name; if it should have the acute accent over the penult (jIounivan) then it is a woman's name... And what they reveal is that jIounian was largely considered a man's name (for the bulk of the MSS have the circumflex over the ultima)." We are also informed that "the man's name Junianas was frequent enough in Latin and Greek writings" while "Iunias also occurred as a masculine name on occasion" (Wallace, "Junia Among the Apostles: The Double Identification Problem in Romans 16:7," Bible.org, http://www.curate.us/s/2r7g [accessed August 12, 2013]; cf. Jones, *A Female Apostle?: A Lexical-Syntactical Analysis of Romans 16:7*). Jones refers to J. A. Fitzmyer's book *Romans*, page 738, which was published by Doubleday in 1993. Several scholars, however, assert that most minuscule manuscripts have Junia(s) accentuated as feminine. Jones explains that others, like Cervin, catalog modern editions of the Greek text and show how they support the feminine reading, while they fail to mention the accentuation in the older minuscules which support the masculine reading. Jones argues that these are closer to the source and constitute more weighty evidence than the later editions. The fact that they have it accented the same, no matter what part of the world they were found in, suggests that the gender issue had been settled some time before. The idea put forward that Junia's gender was being held unanimously as feminine is thus made at the expense of this evidence which suggests otherwise (Jones, *A Female Apostle?: A Lexical-Syntactical Analysis of Romans 16:7*).

It is remarkable that in the 1968 UBS (United Bible Societies) text minuscules are quoted as evidence for the masculine accented 'Iounian' and no feminine form is acknowledged, while, for instance, in 1993, minuscules are given as evidence of the feminine accent while no minuscules are quoted for the masculine. Although the preferred view of many now is that Junia was a female apostle, we should realize how complicated and confusing this issue really is. We should understand that it is rather contestable that Junia was indeed a woman and also an apostle, but if she truly was, she might have been so in the wider sense of the word, or she might have served as such in partnership with her husband. Thus, even if the correct exegesis of Romans 16:7 implies that Andronicus and Junia were themselves apostles, rather than being esteemed by the apostles, it does not mean that Junia, as a woman, was in authority in the church. We should keep in mind that there is no definite evidence on either side, but we may know that a leading feminine apostle does not match biblical and early church historical information.

Concluding this chapter, it is clear that no definite consensus is attained on the exegesis of Romans 16:7. There are hypothetical aspects, debatable theories, assertions and suppositions, while also scribal errors are assumed. During the last decennia, much has been written on this text and it appears more as if Romans 16:7 is like a draw. The different parties can pick and choose what they like most. It is true that interesting things, ably written, have been presented, but neither party can use it to prove their view conclusively. How poorly our position will be when we come to a conclusion based upon a problematic and disputable Bible text. No, this is not the way we should go about to determine truth. What we need is a solid and sound Biblical exegesis of the position of women, straightforwardly based on the clear information of the entire Bible.

Thus, it is clear that those in favor of the ordination of women have only a weak and doubtful case if it is based on this argument about Junia. It is better to dismiss this case, because it cannot be convincingly substantiated on all points. We must conclude that since this dubious issue is a matter of great controversy, it is not wise to try to build a strong case upon Romans 16:7 in favor of ordaining women to positions of responsible leadership in the church.

Chapter 22

Phoebe, A Woman Church Leader?

In his epistle to the Romans the apostle Paul introduces and recommends "Phebe our sister," or Phoebe, "which is a servant of the church which is at Cenchrea" (Rom. 16:1, 2). In the context of the issue over the position of women in the church, the interest in this scriptural passage has been particularly kindled during the last decennium. In what capacity was Phoebe ministering as a servant of the church? Was she a deaconess or was she a responsible leader, or even a minister in the church? The Greek word for "servant" is *diakonos*. The traditional meaning of this word has always been "a servant of someone; a helper or a deacon" (Arndt, *A Greek-English Lexicon of the New Testament*, p. 183).

Paul also uses the word *diakonos* to signify the ministering work of the ordained gospel workers, as for instance in 1 Corinthians 3:5 and 2 Corinthians 3:6: "… hath made us able ministers of the new testament." Thus the suggestion has been raised: Could Phoebe not also have been, in a similar way, a leading servant in the church or a minister of the gospel? However, is it necessary to equate ministry with an office? Is it only possible to serve or minister if one is an appointed officer?

The word *diakonos* does not specify precisely the capacity or position in which the ministering work in the church is performed. Note that the word *diakonos* is, for instance, also used to signify the ministering work of Onesimus, unto Paul as a prisoner (Philemon 10–13). Was Onesimus a church leader? Was he an appointed officer or minister? No, he was a fugitive slave, and so the word *diakonos* does not particularly specify a certain kind of ministry, but it is used in a more general sense, indicating any type of ministry towards fellow men and women within and outside the church.

If we are inclined to regard Phoebe as a leading minister in the church, because of the word *diakonos*, then we must consider that we apply only this possible masculine usage of the word, and ignore the feminine implications. Phoebe, however, is a woman, not a man, and the gospel ministry is not one-sided, but versatile. We are not all called, men and women alike, to do exactly the same work in the same capacity. "There are diversities of gifts … differences of administrations … diversities of operations" (1 Cor. 12:4–6).

We accept then, that *diakonos* has the same meaning for men and women alike, which certainly is not always true. Several New Testament Greek lexicons present a masculine and feminine meaning and refer to Phoebe as a deaconess. For example, Hermann Cremer is very specific in stating: "In Romans 16,1 a woman, Phoebe, is named as *diakonos* … cf. 1 Timothy 5,10 (not v. 9) with Romans 16, 2; 1 Timothy 3, 11, a passage which on indisputable grounds must be taken as referring to Deaconesses" (Cremer, *Biblico-Theological Lexicon of New Testament Greek*, p. 159).

It is also argued that it is remarkable that the word *diakonos* is being used in Romans 16:1 in its masculine form, while a woman is meant. Therefore, to interpret Paul's statement that bishops and deacons must be "the husband of one wife" (1 Tim. 3:2, 12) to mean exclusively that only men can be bishops or deacons, then his statement would be invalid if *diakonos* implies that women can also be appointed.

This argument, however, is not sound because apart from the word *diakonos*, the context of 1 Timothy 3:1–10 is clearly masculine. If we compare it with Titus 1:5–9 a passage with similar import, the masculine context is confirmed. That the word *diakonos* is used in its masculine form is not of any particular meaning, since the early church used this word for both genders with masculine and feminine articles. In Romans 16:1 *diakonos* is used with the feminine participle *oúsan* (accusative singular). When this word became more commonly used, a specific feminine form was introduced: *diaconissa*. This word, however, is also used "to signify not a deaconess, but a deacon's wife" (Bingham, *Origines Ecclesiasticae; or the Antiquities of the Christian Church*, vol. 1, p. 259).

Note also the following quotation: "Servant (*diakonon*). The word may be either masculine or feminine. Commonly explained as deaconess. The term 'diakonissa'—deaconess is found only in ecclesiastical Greek. Their duties were to take care of the sick and poor, to minister to martyrs and confessors in prison, to instruct catechumens, to assist at the baptism of women, and to exercise a general supervision over the female church-members" (Vincent, *Word Studies in the New Testament*, vol. 3, pp. 176, 177).

Another quotation also confirms that a feminine form was not in use until later: "Deaconess, 1. In the Apostolic Age: The function dates from the earliest period of the Church, though the technical term in the feminine form, 'deaconess' (Gk. Diakonissa; Lat. Diaconissa, diaconal), does not occur till a later period. Phoebe was a deaconess in the church of Cenchrea" (Jackson, *The New Schaf-Herzog Encyclopedia of Religious Knowledge*, vol. 3, p. 374).

Therefore, it should not surprise us that the masculine word *diakonos* is applied to a woman. There is no valid reason to use the fact that the word *diakonos* is masculine to argue that women occupied leading positions in the church. Such a conclusion would not be in accordance with the facts as they existed in the early church. There would have to be many other valid and logical indications of this occurrence to prove this practice. Here it is simply a grammar question, not a question of gender, role, or practice.

Joseph Bingham, the author of *Antiquities of the Christian Church*, provides us with reliable information. He wrote, without any bias, a substantial chapter on Deaconesses in the Church, citing early sources. He does not give us any hint that women were responsible leaders in the church. He wrote: "It appears, that their office was as ancient as the apostolic age. St. Paul calls Phoebe, 'a servant of the Church of Cenchrea.' Rom. xvi. 1. The original word is Diakonos, a deaconess, answerable to the Latin word 'Ministra', which is the name that is given them in Pliny's Epistle, which speaks about the Christians" (book 2, p. 247).

We read that their ministry is "to be a decent help to the female sex in the time of their baptism, sickness, affliction, or the like …" (Ibid., p. 255). It is absolutely denied that any woman is ordained to the office of presbyters or priests in the Christian Church, and Bingham continues: "And, from hence it is plain, the offices of the deaconesses were… chiefly relating to the women, for whose sake they were ordained. One part of their office was to assist the minister at the baptizing of women, where, for decency's sake, they were employed to divest them, (the custom, then, being to baptize all adult persons by immersion) and so to order the matter, that the whole ceremony might be performed with all the decency becoming so sacred an action" (Ibid.)

Thus there is no reason at all to suppose that the word *diakonos,* as applied to women, should have indicated a responsible position of church leadership usually reserved for men.

Similarly, another argument is built on the word "succourer" in Romans 16:2, which is also applied to Phoebe. The feminine Greek word is *prostatis,* which is only used here in the New Testament, while the masculine form *prostates* is used some eight times in the Septuagint, the Old Testament in Greek. This masculine word is used as an argument that Phoebe occupied a leading position in the church.

It is indeed true that the masculine form may also indicate leadership, but it does not make sense to illustrate and prove the meaning of this masculine word as such, since it does not necessarily harmonize and correspond, in all its aspects, to the feminine word and its meaning. If we look it up, for instance, in Edward Robinson's *A Greek and English Lexicon of the New Testament,* we find a noteworthy difference between the feminine and masculine words: "*prostatis* - a patroness, protectress, *adjutrix,* Rom. 16:2. – The masc. form is *prostates,* i.e. one who presides, a leader, *antistes*" (p. 651). According to *Cassell's New Latin Dictionary, adjutrix* means "she that helps, a female assistant, a helper" (p. 15). Thus it seems that the feminine word *prostatis* is not exactly identical with the masculine *prostates.* While the feminine word could indicate a helper or assistant, the masculine could denote a presiding officer.

However, it seems also plausible that the choice of a masculine or feminine form of the word would emphasize the action more than the person who acts. Therefore, *prostatis* would mean "one who helps," and the masculine, "one who leads." So it could be meant that Phoebe was a "succourer," one who leads in helping, which, apparently, would be true.

Ethelbert Bullinger lists the following words for the masculine form: "a presider, prefect, magistrate, curator, guardian, patron" and for the feminine word: "a patroness, helper, succourer" (Bullinger, *A Critical Lexicon and Concordance to the English and Greek New Testament,* p. 747). W. E. Vine says that the feminine prostatis "denotes a protectress, patroness; it is used metaphorically of Phoebe in Rom. 16:2. It is a word of dignity" (Vine, *The Expanded Vine's Expository Dictionary of New Testament Words*, p. 1101).

Did Paul, by using the word *prostatis*, really mean that Phoebe was a leader? If this were true, Romans 16:2 would read "she hath been a leader of many, and of myself also." Do we really believe that Phoebe was a leader over Paul? But Paul did not say that she was a leader of the church. Instead, he said that Phoebe was a *helper, patroness, or succourer,* the feminine means, which fits the context properly and makes sense.

Note also this quote: "That Phoebe is being called a leader here is improbable for three reasons. (1) It is highly improbable that Paul would say that Phoebe held a position of authority over him … (2) There seems to be a play on words between the word prostatis and the previous verb, paristemi, in 16:2. Paul says to help (paristemi) Phoebe because she has been a help (prostatis) to many, including to Paul himself. It fits the context better to understand Paul as saying 'help Phoebe because she has been such a help to others and to me.' (3) Although the related masculine noun prostatēs can mean 'leader,' the actual feminine noun (prostatis) does not take the meaning 'leader' but is defined as 'protectress, patroness, helper'" (Piper, *Recovering Biblical Manhood & Womanhood*, pp. 219, 220).

Since Phoebe was a woman, it would not be wise to suggest her position in the church with masculine words, because we might then arrive at conclusions that are far from the truth. If it is clear that the word *diakonos,* as applied to women, does not imply responsible leadership in the church, which apparently is the case, then it should not be expected that in the second verse Phoebe's leadership is implied. That assumption would be out of harmony with the first verse, unless Phoebe was thought of as a "leader in helping."

If it were true that Phoebe was a leader, ruler, bishop, or elder in the church, why did Paul not say so in a direct and straightforward way, using appropriate words, such as *proistemi,* 1 Timothy 5:17; or *hegeomai,* Hebrews 13:7, 17, 24; or *episcopos* or *presbuteros,* 1 Timothy 3:1, 2 and Titus 1:5, 7? Paul was not a mysterious or misleading man. No, he was inspired by the Holy Spirit who enabled him to select the most expressive language. And so, if Phoebe was really a church leader, Paul, moved by the Holy Spirit, certainly would have said so plainly in his recommendation to the Roman Christians, rather than being obscure about Phoebe's real position in the church. Even if Phoebe's leadership were somehow an exception to the rule, one would think that Paul would also have mentioned that fact, as he would not have wanted to confuse his listeners and readers as to how to organize the church.

We don't know much about Phoebe. Does the word *prostatis* relate to her work as a deaconess in the church? Or did she perhaps serve a similar role in society, outside the church? If that is true and the word *prostatis* is a reference to that role, then it is unnecessary to argue that this word might suggest that she was a leader in the church. Did Phoebe go to Rome for some kind of private business, taking Paul's letter to the Roman Christians with her? It is possible, but we don't precisely know.

According to *The Expositor's Greek Testament*, Paul could have used, with regard to Phoebe, the word *parastatis* (a female helper), but he used the more honorable word *prostates* (patronus) which was the title of a citizen in Athens who took charge of the interests of strangers and persons without civic rights, while "the corresponding feminine here may suggest that Phoebe was a woman of good position ..." (Ibid., vol. 2, p. 718). If Paul indeed uses the word *prostatis* only because it was more honorable, why should we try to introduce another reason to signify that Phoebe occupied a leading role in the church?

Note John Gill's comment: "The word that is here used ... is, as Harpocratian says, the name by which such were called by the Athenians ... that were over the sojourners, who had the care and direction of them. And such was this woman to the poor ... and the strangers ...; not as being in such an office by the order and appointment of the church, but what she cheerfully and voluntarily took up herself, and performed at her own expense, otherwise there would not be so much in the character as to deserve such peculiar notice, nor she be so worthy of praise and commendation" (Gill, *Gill's Commentary*, vol. 6, pp. 141, 142).

Note also Patrick Fairbairn's observation: "St. Paul commends her as having been 'a succourer of many, and of himself also:' having been so helpful to others in the best of causes, it was meet that she should herself receive help in so far as she might need it. But she might have been and done all this without holding any office in the church; and it is a question whether, when she is designated 'a servant (diakonos) of the church,...' the apostle means simply an active member, or one in the position of a deaconess" (Fairbairn, *Fairbairn's Imperial Standard Bible Encyclopedia, Historical, Biographical, Geographical and Doctrinal*, vol. 5, p. 249).

In the opinion of several scholars, Phoebe did not occupy a prominent position in the church. Rather, she was honored for holding a charitable position. Although this assumption could be correct, in general the information about Phoebe is scanty. This being so, a door is opened for our imagination and, unfortunately, too often unproved suggestions and theories find their way into our reasoning. However, since there is no solid evidence available, we must conclude that the view of Phoebe as a church leader extends the interpretation too far beyond the information we have. Such a view is out of harmony with Paul's specific teaching about the position and role of women, and it is also inconsistent with early church history.

Ellen White simply explains, "Phebe entertained the apostle, and she was in a marked manner an entertainer of strangers who needed care. Her example should be followed by the churches of today" (White, *Testimonies for the Church*, vol. 6, p. 344). This is a clear statement, and it is not wise to go beyond that, trying to maneuver Phoebe somehow in a prominent leadership role in the church. We should never build our faith on a disputed foundation with suggestions and insights that are not truly demonstrable, nor in full harmony with the Bible.

Chapter 23

Women Who Can Manage a Church?

A few people argue that Ellen White has suggested that dedicated, faithful women could be appointed as leaders in the church which would obviate the question of ordaining consecrated women. To support their claim, they refer to a short statement headed with these words: "Women Who Can Manage a Church," where Ellen White writes: "It is not always men who are best adapted to the successful management of a church. If faithful women have more deep piety and true devotion than men, they could indeed by their prayers and their labors do more than men who are unconsecrated in heart and in life" (White, *Manuscript Release*, vol. 10, p. 70).

The accent in this short passage is on women who are truly devoted in contrast with unconsecrated men. This statement portrays on the one side a church in need of stronger, more dedicated management where unconsecrated men are in leadership, and on the other side the prevailing prayers and labors of faithful, pious women. Although the title could suggest women's leadership in the church, the statement is not directive on this issue.

It must be emphasized that God does not work exclusively through men alone. Women are often chosen by God or impressed by the Holy Spirit to take strong action in a church where such consecration is lacking. God can often work much better through dedicated, pious women than through unconsecrated men. The principle here is that consecration is a necessary feature to serve the church successfully. Ellen White has also pointed out in other statements that devoted, faithful women can do a work in the church that men cannot do, even when they are fully consecrated. Thus, the church is built not only by men but most surely also by women, and the more so by consecrated women, rather than by unconsecrated men.

Ellen White does not speak in this passage about devoted women being called to leadership in the church or being ordained as pastors. She simply makes clear that devoted women, by their prayers and labors, can do more in the church than will be achieved by the management of unconsecrated men. It is the prerogative of every faithful believer, either man or woman, to build the church by prayer and labor. Ellen White uses the word "management" in relation to men, and in relation to faithful women, she uses the words "prayers and labors." She emphasizes that godly women can do more in the church than unconsecrated men. She did not specify that pious women can do more as ordained leaders in the church. She specified that they can do more by their prayers and labors.

As for the title of this passage, "Women Who Can Manage a Church," we should keep in mind that it was not Ellen White who wrote this heading. Those who compiled her statements provided the titles to classify the various passages and make a quick and accurate overview possible. Therefore, a meaning that is suggested by a title cannot be attributed to Ellen White. Even so, we can ask in what sense faithful women are meant to manage a church. Did the editors in choosing this title, or perhaps Ellen White in writing her statement, intend to say that dedicated, pious women could rule the church as ordained leaders, with full ecclesiastical authority? Would it not be true that such an intention will be beyond the scope of this particular statement? The passage itself does not clearly indicate such a thought and, therefore, we should be careful not to draw an unwarranted conclusion.

In her writings, Ellen White has specified clearly in what fields and capacity women can do a blessed work in the church. It would be more commendable to understand and explain her statements harmoniously. Introducing unintended meanings or possible implications out of harmony with her other writings can only bring further conflict to this sensitive issue.

Chapter 24

Women Not Permitted to Speak?

The apostle Paul wrote to the Corinthian church: "Let your women keep silence in the churches: for it is not permitted unto them to speak; but they are commanded to be under obedience, as also saith the law" (1 Cor. 14:34).

To many people these words are rather difficult to understand and some, in their zeal for obedience to God's word, have ruled out all women's activity in the church. It would be beneficial, therefore, to pay due attention to this counsel. What is the meaning of this passage? Are women not allowed to say a word in the church? What is the background of issuing this instruction?

Some time ago I attended a Sabbath School where a woman in the class did most of the talking. The teacher had hardly said or asked something when this woman got up to speak again. Consequently, there was not much of a chance for others to also say something. At a certain moment, when the teacher had addressed the class again with a question, he immediately turned to this woman and said: "You must be silent." Did the teacher mean by these words that this woman was not allowed to say a word in Sabbath School anymore? Did he mean that this woman should always be silent when she attended a class? Obviously not. It is clear that the teacher wanted this woman to realize that she could not monopolize the discussion, thus giving others no opportunity to say something. Evidently something similar was also happening in the church of Corinth.

In the days of the apostle Paul, the seaport Corinth was a great commercial center. People from all over the world crowded into its streets. The church was infected by a situation that resulted in an atmosphere of loose morals, much idolatry, and immorality. It is generally known that the church of Corinth was out of balance: it had many problems and it was divided by discord. Surrounded by idolatry and the pursuit of sensual pleasure in the most seductive forms, many had become careless, light-hearted, and indifferent. The people had even returned to some degrading pagan habits. They indulged their natural lusts and inclinations, and although they had become believers, some liberal, emancipated women dressed immodestly and did not behave respectably or respectfully in church. A loose, pleasure-seeking, shallow attitude, usually so common in a thriving seaport, was also exhibited in the church, resulting in a disorderly service.

Reproof was necessary, so the apostle Paul directed his reproof and instructions to the Corinthian church. He wrote: "How is it then, brethren? when ye come together, every one of you hath a psalm, hath a doctrine, hath a tongue, hath a revelation, hath an interpretation. Let all things be done unto edifying" (1 Cor. 14:26). To preserve order in the church, the apostle instructed that only two or three people should speak in tongues, in due course, with an interpreter. If there was no interpreter, there should be silence (verses 27, 28). Two or three prophets could speak in turn, while the others should listen and think it over. When a revelation comes to another who is seated, he should share the message after the others are finished speaking. All may, each in turn, give a testimony, that all might learn and be comforted. Paul stresses that "God is not the author of confusion, but of peace" (verse 33).

Then the apostle admonishes: "Let your women keep silence in the churches" (verse 34a). The context in which this passage is written, justifies the conclusion that the Corinthian church meeting was not orderly. Evidently, some spoke while others were still speaking, not waiting for their turn. And evidently, there were women speaking not only out of turn but also, perhaps, in a bold or immodest way. We don't precisely know if they were preaching or talking, or if they were assuming a leading role, as the woman in Sabbath School did. (See my anecdote above.) Possibly all these aspects may have existed in the Corinthian church. Paul reminded them: "For it is not permitted unto them [the women] to speak; but they are commanded to be under obedience, as also saith the law. And if they will learn any thing, let them ask their husbands at home: for it is a shame for women to speak in the church" (verse 34b).

Asking questions during the service could not only cause some delay, but easily start a disorderly discussion in such a divided community as the Corinthian church was. Such a discussion could disrupt the meeting and also defeat the purpose of worship. The apostle instructs these women, therefore, to ask and discuss their questions in the home circle. After this directive statement, he adds the strong words: "For it is a shame for women to speak in the church" (verse 35). The way the people behaved in church was not commendable, so the apostle urged the Corinthian believers: "Let all things be done decently and in order" (verse 40). The problem of disorder in the Corinthian church definitely creates a context for Paul's counsel to the women.

The apostle states that women "are commanded to be under obedience [be in subjection] as also saith the law" (verse 34). Evidently some women in the Corinthian church were not behaving as if they were in subjection but were stepping outside "the law" of subjection. We remember that Ellen White says that after the fall Eve "was ... placed in subjection to her husband" (White, *Patriarchs and Prophets*, p. 58). According to this law, a woman should not pride herself in doing much of the talking or teaching in church. The apostle does not allow that, as is also indicated by other passages. Does this mean that a woman is not allowed to say a word in the church? Should she be absolutely silent? Was that Paul's intention as he wrote his counsel to the churches? No, certainly not. Paul had spoken earlier of women praying and prophesying in the church (1 Cor. 11:5). Here the apostle is emphasizing that there should be behavior and order in the church (verses 33, 40). Women may speak in church in a decent, modest, and becoming way within the scope indicated by Scripture.

Note that Paul refers to the law, commanding women to be under obedience or in subjection. We must assume that this law of submission (Gen. 3:16) is still in force in New Testament times, or the apostle's reference would be meaningless, for it is not possible to support something with a law that has been abrogated. The apostle addresses behavioral proceedings *in the church* and thus the law referred to is not only in force in the home circle, but also in the church where a woman should behave in a similar, modest way. The same law of subjection can be applied to the possibility of ordaining women elders and ministers. It is clear that this law of submission is still in force after Christ's redeeming death on Calvary's cross.

Near the end of this biblical passage that we have examined, the apostle assures us: "The things that I write unto you are the commandments of the

Lord" (verse 37). Should we then consider Paul's rules from a popular viewpoint? Should we adjust the biblical instructions to the modern principles of our society? Biblical principles have never matched the world's way of thinking and so we must choose. There is no doubt that we would do well to take Paul's instructions seriously, as commanded by God.

Chapter 25

Bible Truth or Cultural Values?

The whole Bible is the revealed will of God. Therefore it is always wise to compare Bible passages on a certain subject throughout the whole Bible. With regard to fundamental Bible truth, we always refer, as responsible students of the Bible, to events, circumstances and situations as existing at the beginning of this world.

A few clear examples may illustrate this:

- With respect to the Sabbath, we refer to the Creation week when the Sabbath was instituted: Genesis 2:1, 2.
- When we explain the mortality of the soul, we refer to Genesis 2:17.
- When speaking of the atonement through the law of offering, we refer to Genesis 3:21.
- When we consider the institution of marriage, we look at the relationship between man and woman as they were created: Genesis 2:22.
- When we consider the great controversy between good and evil or between Christ and Satan, we look at Genesis 3:15.
- To illustrate true and false forms of worship we refer to the offerings of Cain and Abel in Genesis 4:4, 5.
- When presenting our health message we go to the beginning where God prescribed our original diet in Genesis 1:29.
- As we talk about the kingdom of grace, we go back to the beginning when it was instituted, right after the fall: Genesis 3 and Ellen White, *The Great Controversy*, p. 347.

- We go to the beginning as we are confronted with the subject of evolution: Genesis 1 and 2.
- To proclaim the three angels' messages, we refer to the beginning to call on people to worship the Creator: Genesis 1and 2.
- To understand the power of temptation and to discern Satan's sophistry, we turn to the beginning to contemplate how Eve was misled: Genesis 3:1–6.
- To determine the future of this world and the purpose of life we go back to the beginning to consider God's original plan for the human race and for the world: Genesis 1–3.
- As we study God's plan of redemption, we refer back to the beginning when it was set in operation after the fall: Genesis 3:15.
- If we really want to obtain a correct Biblical understanding of any important subject, we go back to the beginning. God's last day message of salvation and God's plan for our preparation for Jesus' second coming is rooted in the beginning of His Word.

In the context of the issue of women's ordination, even when we see that Eve was formed from Adam's rib to be a helpmate for him and even when we understand that she was not intended to be a head, ruler or authoritative leader with great responsibility, many people will ignore Biblical truth. Instead, they will embrace the egalitarian principles of modern culture.

The apostle Paul, in clear contrast to this attitude, follows the truth. With respect to the position of women and their relationship to men, he refers faithfully to Creation (1 Cor. 11:8, 9; 1 Tim. 2:13); to the fall (1 Tim. 2:14); and to the law of subordination, pronounced by God to Eve right after the fall, as a consequence of her sin (1 Cor. 14:34; Gen. 3:16). Jesus in His teaching also recognized the authority of the truth as it existed from the beginning (Matt. 19:4, 8). When we turn to the beginning, we learn a number of important aspects of truth concerning the position of Adam and Eve.

Adam's pre-eminence. Adam was created first. He was placed in the Garden of Eden and given instructions. The privilege of giving names to every living creature was granted to him. Then Eve was made, taken out of man to be his helper (Gen. 2:7–23). The Hebrew word "ezer", in verse 18, clearly means:

aid, help, succour. The Septuagint records the Greek word "boèthos" which also means helper. The position of Eve, and her relationship to Adam, as all wives to all husbands, should therefore be clear. There is no need to have any doubt about that. Note how Ellen White aptly specifies Eve as "a helper corresponding to him" (White, *The Adventist Home*, p. 25).

A sample of all families. In another statement, Ellen White makes clear that the first human family, Adam and Eve, served as an example for all human families of all ages.

Note what she says: "The Lord calls upon all to study the divine philosophy of sacred history, written by Moses under inspiration of the Holy Spirit. The first family placed upon the earth is a sample of all families which will exist till the close of time" (White, *Manuscript Releases*, vol. 3, p. 184).

The Lord tells us here that the first family, Adam and Eve, serves as a model for all families on earth until the close of time. Thus, it is clear that the relationship of Adam and Eve, with Eve as Adam's helper, is still a relevant pattern for every human family. Since the church is analogous to the family, "every family is a church" (White, *Child Guidance*, p. 549), the same biblical principles exist in both home and church. Thus, a woman's ordination in the church as elder or pastor will place her in an inappropriate position of headship and leadership. Instead of being a helper, she will then be a head and leader.

Protecting influence. Note also how Eve was cautioned "to beware of separating herself from her husband" (White, *Patriarchs and Prophets*, p. 53). This counsel is significant. Adam's presence would be a protecting influence against temptation. She would be in less danger near Adam than if she were alone. (Ibid.)

Adam was Lord. Furthermore, consider that Ellen White suggests that in Eden, before the fall, there was a difference in relation between Adam and Eve. Adam is particularly specified as being lord; therefore both possessed Eden with a functional difference between them: "Adam and Eve were rich indeed. They possessed Eden. Adam was lord in his beautiful domain" (White, *Fundamentals of Christian Education*, p. 38).

King–Sovereign–Vicegerent–Father–Representative–Head. "Adam was crowned as king in Eden … He made Adam the rightful sovereign over all the works of His hands" (White, *Review and Herald*, February 24, 1874). "Adam was the vicegerent of the Creator" (White, *The Desire of Ages*, p. 129).

"The Sabbath was committed to Adam, the father and representative of the whole human family" (White, *Patriarchs and Prophets*, p. 48). "Under God, Adam was to stand at the head of the earthly family to maintain the principles of the heavenly family" (White, *Testimonies for the Church*, vol. 6, p. 236). Thus Adam's pre-eminence is clearly illustrated.

Before the fall there was no need to specifically declare Adam's headship and authority, since there was perfect love and harmony. The first couple in Eden had daily communion with God and with the holy angels. They were directed and guided by the Holy Spirit without any sense of envy or competition.

Adam's primary responsibility. When Adam and Eve sinned, it is recorded that "the Lord God called unto Adam, and said unto him, Where art thou" (Gen. 3:9). Adam was called, although "Adam was not deceived, but the woman being deceived was in the transgression" (1 Tim. 2:14). Adam, in his fall, was moved by another principle: "His love for Eve was strong. And in utter discouragement he resolved to share her fate" (White, *The Story of Redemption*, p. 36). In spite of Eve being the first offender, Adam bore the primary responsibility, and thus, Paul denotes Adam as the *one man*, who brought sin into the world and Christ as the *one* who brought grace, righteousness and eternal life into the world (Rom. 5:12, 15).

Significant factors. The fact that Adam had to take the responsibility for the first sin, rather than Eve, and that Christ is the second Adam, are significant and meaningful factors, not to be neglected. Note the implication of Adam's position in the context of the fall and the atoning work of Christ: "Christ is called the second Adam … He began where the first Adam began. Willingly He passed over the ground where Adam fell, and redeemed Adam's failure" (White, *My Life Today*, p. 323). "But Christ, by His sacrifice paying the penalty of sin, would not only redeem man, but recover the dominion which he had forfeited. All that was lost by the first Adam will be restored by the second" (White, *Patriarchs and Prophets*, p. 67).

Adam re-installed. When Christ invites His redeemed people to enter the New Jerusalem, "The two Adams are about to meet. The Son of God is standing with outstretched arms to receive the father of our race … The Son of God redeemed man's failure and fall; and now, through the work of the atonement, Adam is reinstated in his first dominion" (White, *The Great Controversy*, pp. 647, 648).

False theory. The theory that it was only after sin that the woman was placed under male headship is false. Thus the gospel purpose is not to restore a non-headship relationship of man to woman, in which there is equality of function and office.

Functional differences. The way Adam and Eve are presented and described, as well as the prominent place Adam occupied in several respects, and also the characteristics particularly attributed to him, indicate a difference from Eve in position, authority and responsibility, resulting in functional differences between them.

This model for the correct relationship between men and women, however, is not in harmony with modern culture where men and women are regarded to be equal, without differences in function and role, and where women, just like men, should have access to any office or function of leadership. This principle of equality is not supported in the Bible. To every sincere Christian it should be clear that the Bible does not sanction functional equality between men and women; nor does the Bible sanction female ordination on an equal basis with a male, since, as we have seen before, any precedent for this is lacking in God's Word.

Preserving unity. It is usually not the great majority of church members who actually wish or insist on female leadership. It is usually the desire of a few leaders in the church to ordain women in positions of leadership. Some churches are even openly against such an action while in other churches this issue creates much strife and discord. It certainly would be wise to preserve unity and faithfully follow the biblical rule.

An important question. In the book of Job a very important question is asked, "He is wise in heart, and mighty in strength: who hath hardened himself against him, and hath prospered?" Job 9:4. The Berkeley version says: "…who could resist Him without harm?" Going back in human history we notice that man, right from the very beginning, has ventured to resist God. The woman saw that the forbidden tree was good for food and she did eat and much harm, misery and death was the result. Cain was warned against sin, but he resisted God and he became the first murderer and was cursed. The people in Noah's days resisted God's message and they all perished in the flood. After the flood God commanded the people to replenish the earth, but they cherished other plans. They built a city with a tower and their speech was confused. Lot and his family on their escape was admonished not to look behind, but Lot's wife looked back and she became a pillar of salt. And so, throughout the ages there have been men and women who resisted the words of God and had to face the harmful results.

The apostle Paul, after he had given his instructions and specified the position of women in the church, declared distinctly and very meaningful, "If any man think himself to be a prophet, or spiritual, let him acknowledge that the things that I write unto you are the commandments of the Lord" (1 Cor. 14:37). Thus, we should realize that if we are at variance with Paul's teaching regarding the position of women in the church we are at variance with God's commandments, and consequently, we are confronted with that impressive question, "… who hath hardened himself against him, and hath prospered?" (Job. 9:4). Resisting God's plain words will certainly bring harmful results. And let it be remembered that all which is built upon the authority of man will be overthrown, but the things founded upon the rock of God's unchanging Word will remain forever.

A firm stand. We should bear in mind that our message is not in every detail very popular in this world. Some aspects are in conflict with the principles of modern society and the culture of today. In these areas the ultimate choices are Bible culture or secular worldly culture. The choice of Abel or the choice of Cain. A compromise will not do. Once the door has been opened just a little, it may soon be opened further. We should be very careful not to neglect even one small aspect of truth, for it would then be all too easy to surrender other aspects of the truth. A decidedly firm stand, unyielding as a rock, in defense of biblical truth is most assuredly always urgent and very necessary. May the Lord help us to make right choices as we choose to serve Him acceptably.

Bibliography

Alford, Henry. *The Greek Testament.* 4 vols. Rivingtons, London, Oxford and Cambridge: Deighton, Bell, and Co., 1865.

Arndt, William F., and F. Wilbur Gingrich. *A Greek-English Lexicon of the New Testament and Other Early Christian Literature.* Cambridge and Chicago, IL: The University of Chicago Press, Fourth Impression, 1959.

Barnes, Albert. *Notes on the New Testament.* 14 vols. Grand Rapids, MI: Baker Books, 2001.

Barnes, Albert, and H. C. Leupold. *Exposition on Genesis in 2 Volumes.* Vol. I. Baker, 1942.

Bengel, John Albert. *New Testament Word Studies.* 2 vols. Grand Rapids, MI: Kregel Publications, 1971.

Benson, Joseph. *The Holy Bible Containing the Old and New Testaments: With Critical, Explanatory, and Practical Notes.* Vol. III. J. Mason, 1815.

Bingham, Joseph. *Origines Ecclesiasticae, or the Antiquities of the Christian Church and Other Works.* 8 vols. London: William Straker, 1834.

Bullinger, Ethelbert. *A Critical Lexicon and Concordance to the English and Greek New Testament.* 11th ed. London: Samuel Bagster and Sons Limited, 1974.

Burer, Michael H. "Was Junia Really an Apostle? A Reexamination of Romans 16:7." *Journal of Biblical Manhood and Womanhood,* Fall 2001.

Bradnock, W. J., and H. K. Moulton, trans. *The Translator's New Testament.* London: The British and Foreign Bible Society, 1973.

Cheyne, T. K., and J. Sutherland Black, eds. *Encyclopaedia Biblica.* 4 vols. London: Adam and Charles Black, 1914.

Cremer, Hermann. *Biblico-Theological Lexicon of New Testament Greek.* Edinburgh: T & T Clark, 1872.

Dummelow, J. R., ed. *A Commentary on the Holy Bible by Various Writers.* London: Macmillan and Co., Ltd, 1909.

Erdman, Charles R. *The Pastoral Epistles of Paul.* Philadelphia, PA: The Westminster Press, 1925.

Fairbairn, Patrick. *Fairbairn's Imperial Standard Bible Encyclopedia, Historical, Biographical, Geographical and Doctrinal.* Grand Rapids, MI: Zondervan Publishing House, 1957.

Fallows, Samuel, ed. *The Popular and Critical Bible Encyclopaedia and Scriptural Dictionary, Fully Defining and Explaining All Religious Terms.* 3 vols. Chicago, IL: The Howard-Severance Company, 1914.

Fitzmyer, Joseph A, *Romans,* Anchor Bible, Volume 33, Garden City, N.Y. Doubleday, 1993.

Gill, John. *Gill's Commentary.* 6 vols. Grand Rapids, MI: Baker Book House, 1980.

Gore, Charles, Henry Leighton Goudge, and Alfred Guillaume, eds. *A New Commentary on Holy Scripture, including the Apocrypha.* London: Society for Promoting Christian Knowledge, 1928.

Graffin, R and F. Nau, Patrologia Orientalis, *Tomus Decimus Sextus,* (vol. 16) Chapter II, René Basset, Le Synaxaire Arabe Jacobite, Paris: Firmin-Didot, 1922.

Hardinge, Leslie. *With Jesus in His Sanctuary.* Harrisburg, PA: American Cassette Ministries, Book Division, 1991.

Harris, R. Laird, Gleason L. Archer, and Bruce K. Waltke, eds. *Theological Wordbook of the Old Testament.* Chicago: Moody Press, 1980.

Hastings, James, ed. John A. Selbie and John C. Lambert, assist. eds. *Dictionary of the Apostolic Church.* 2 vols. Edinburgh: T. & T. Clark, 1915.

Hastings, James, ed. John A. Selbie and John C. Lambert, assist. eds. *Encyclopaedia of Religion and Ethics.* 13 vols. Edinburgh: T. & T. Clark, 1915.

Jackson, Samuel Macauley, ed. *The New Schaff-Herzog Encyclopedia of Religious Knowledge.* 12 vols. New York and London: Funk and Wagnalls Company, 1909.

Jamieson, Robert, A. R. Fausset, and David Brown. *A Commentary Critical, Experimental and Practical on the Old and New Testaments.* Grand Rapids, MI: Wm. B. Eerdmans Publishing Co., 1945.

Jones, David. *A Female Apostle?: A Lexical-Syntactical Analysis of Romans 16:7.* Wheaton, IL: The Council for Biblical Manhood and Womanhood, 1997.

Kretzmann, Paul E. *The Popular Commentary of the Bible, Old Testament.* Vol. I. 1921.

Kretzmann, Paul E. *The Popular Commentary of the Bible.* Vol. II. St. Louis, MO: Concordia Publ. House, 1923.

Lange, John Peter, *Genesis or the First Book of Moses,* transl. by Tayler Lewis and A. Gosman, Edinburgh, T. & T. Clark, 1868.

Migne, J. P. *Patrologia Graeca.* Vol. 14. Paris: Imprimerie Catholique, 1857–1866.

Moore, Peter, ed. *Man, Woman, and Priesthood.* London: SPCK, 1978.

Nicoll, William Robertson. *The Expositor's Greek Testament.* 5 vols. Grand Rapids, MI: Wm. B. Eerdmans Publishing Co., 1960.

Orr, James, ed. John L. Nuelsen and Edgar Y. Mullins, assist. eds. Morris O. Evans, man. ed. *The International Bible Encyclopaedia.* 5 vols. Chicago, IL: The Howard-Severance Company, 1915.

Piper, John, and Wayne Grudem. *Recovering Biblical Manhood & Womanhood.* Wheaton, IL: Crossway Books, 1991.

Robinson, Edward. *A Greek and English Lexicon of the New Testament.* Andover: Codman Press, 1825.

Schaff, Philip, ed. *A Select Library of the Nicene and Post-Nicene Fathers of the Christian Church.* 14 vols. Buffalo, NY: The Christian Literature Co., 1886–1890.

Schulz, R. R. "Romans 16:7, Junia or Junias?" *The Expository Times: International Journal of Biblical Studies, Theology and Ministry* 98 (1987).

Simpson, D. P., ed. *Cassell's New Latin Dictionary.* New York: Funk & Wagnalls, Macmillan Publishing Company, 1959.

Spence, H. D. M., and Joseph S. Exell. *The Pulpit Commentary.* 23 vols. Grand Rapids, MI: Wm. B. Eerdmans Publishing Co., 1962.

Strong, James. *The Exhaustive Concordance of the Bible.* London: Hodder and Stoughton, 1910.

Thayer, Joseph Henry. *A Greek-English Lexicon of the New Testament, being Grimm's Wilke's Clavis Novi Testamenti.* 4th ed. Edinburgh: T & T Clark, 1961.

The Twentieth Century New Testament, A Translation into Modern English. New York and Chicago: Horace Marshall & Son, London; The Fleming H. Revell Company, 1901.

Vincent, Marvin R. *Word Studies in the New Testament.* 4 vols. Grand Rapids, MI: Wm. B. Eerdmans Publishing Co., 1973.

Vine, W. E. *The Expanded Vine's Expository Dictionary of New Testament Words.* Minneapolis, MN: Bethany House Publishers, 1984.

Wallace, Daniel B, *Junia Among the Apostles: The Double Identification Problem in Romans 16:7,* published June 24th, 2004, at http://www.curate.us/s/2r7g (accessed August 12, 2013).

Weymouth, Richard Francis. *The New Testament in Modern Speech.* London: James Clarke & Co., Ltd., 1926.

White, Ellen G. *The Acts of the Apostles.* Mountain View, CA: Pacific Press Publishing Association, 1911.

White, Ellen G. *The Adventist Home.* Hagerstown, MD: Review and Herald Publishing Association, 1952.

White, Ellen G. *Child Guidance.* Washington, DC: Review and Herald Publishing Association, 1954.

White, Ellen G. *Christ's Object Lessons.* Review and Herald Publishing Association, 1900.

White, Ellen G. *Conflict and Courage.* Washington, DC: Review and Herald Publishing Association, 1970.

White, Ellen G. *Counsels to Parents, Teachers, and Students.* Mountain View, CA: Pacific Press Publishing Association, 1913.

White, Ellen G. *Counsels to Writers and Editors.* Nashville, TN: Southern Publishing Association, 1946.

White, Ellen G. *The Desire of Ages.* Mountain View, CA: Pacific Press Publishing Association, 1898.

White, Ellen G. *Early Writings.* Washington, DC: Review and Herald Publishing Association, 1882.

White, Ellen G. *The Faith I Live By.* Washington, DC: Review and Herald Publishing Association, 1958.

White, Ellen G. *Fundamentals of Christian Education.* Nashville, TN: Southern

Publishing Association, 1923.

White, Ellen G. *The Great Controversy 1888*. Mountain View, CA: Pacific Press Publishing Association, 1888.

White, Ellen G. *The Great Controversy*. Mountain View, CA: Pacific Press Publishing Association, 1911.

White, Ellen G. *Gospel Workers*. Washington, DC: Review and Herald Publishing Association, 1915.

White, Ellen G. *Manuscript Releases*. Vol. 3. Silver Spring, MD: Ellen G. White Estate, 1990.

White, Ellen G. *Manuscript Releases*. Vol. 5. Silver Spring, MD: Ellen G. White Estate, 1990.

White, Ellen G. *Manuscript Releases*. Vol. 10. Silver Spring, MD: Ellen G. White Estate, 1990.

White, Ellen G. *Manuscript Releases*. Vol. 16. Silver Spring, MD: Ellen G. White Estate, 1990.

White, Ellen G. *Manuscript Releases*. Vol. 21. Silver Spring, MD: Ellen G. White Estate, 1993.

White, Ellen G. *My Life Today*. Washington, DC: Review and Herald Publishing Association, 1952.

White, Ellen G. *Patriarchs and Prophets*. Washington, DC: Review and Herald Publishing Association, 1890.

White, Ellen G. *The Paulson Collection of Ellen G. White Letters*. Payson, AZ: Leaves of Autumn Books, 1985.

White, Ellen G. *Prophets and Kings*. Mountain View, CA: Pacific Press Publishing Association, 1917.

White, Ellen G. *Reflecting Christ*. Hagerstown, MD: Review and Herald Publishing Association, 1985.

White, Ellen G. *The SDA Bible Commentary*. Vol. 4. Washington, DC: Review and Herald Publishing Association, 1955.

White, Ellen G. *The SDA Bible Commentary*. Vol. 5. Washington, DC: Review and Herald Publishing Association, 1956.

White, Ellen G. *The SDA Bible Commentary*. Vol. 6. Washington, DC: Review and Herald Publishing Association, 1956.

White, Ellen G. *The SDA Bible Commentary*. Vol. 7. Washington, DC: Review and Herald Publishing Association, 1957.

White, Ellen G. *Selected Messages*. Book 1. Washington, DC: Review and Herald Publishing Association, 1958.

White, Ellen G. *Sons and Daughters of God*. Washington, DC: Review and Herald Publishing Association, 1955.

White, Ellen G. *Spiritual Gifts*. Vol. 4b. Battle Creek, MI: Seventh-day Adventist Publishing Association, 1864.

White, Ellen G. *The Story of Redemption*. Hagerstown, MD: Review and Herald Publishing Association, 1947.

White, Ellen G. *Testimonies for the Church*. Vol. 1. Mountain View, CA: Pacific Press Publishing Association, 1868.

White, Ellen G. *Testimonies for the Church*. Vol. 3. Mountain View, CA: Pacific Press Publishing Association, 1875.

White, Ellen G. *Testimonies for the Church*. Vol. 4. Mountain View, CA: Pacific Press Publishing Association, 1881.

White, Ellen G. *Testimonies for the Church*. Vol. 6. Mountain View, CA: Pacific Press Publishing Association, 1901.

White, Ellen G. *The Upward Look*. Washington, DC: Review and Herald Publishing Association, 1982.

We invite you to view the complete
selection of titles we publish at:

www.TEACHServices.com

Scan with your mobile
device to go directly
to our website.

Please write or email us your praises, reactions, or
thoughts about this or any other book we publish at:

P.O. Box 954
Ringgold, GA 30736

info@TEACHServices.com

TEACH Services, Inc., titles may be purchased in bulk for
educational, business, fund-raising, or sales promotional use.
For information, please e-mail:

BulkSales@TEACHServices.com

Finally, if you are interested in seeing
your own book in print, please contact us at

publishing@TEACHServices.com

We would be happy to review your manuscript for free.

www.ingramcontent.com/pod-product-compliance
Lightning Source LLC
Chambersburg PA
CBHW070051120426
42742CB00048B/2396